Equipped: Activated and Released
Steven Anderson

Equipped: Activated and Released by Steven Anderson

Copyright © Steven Anderson 2021

All rights reserved. This book is protected by copyright laws of the United Kingdom. This book may not be copied or reprinted for commercial gain or profit. The use of short quotations or occasional page copying for personal or group study is permitted and encouraged. Permission will be granted upon request.

Unless otherwise stated, Scripture quotations are from the New American Standard Bible.
Copyright 1996 The Lockman Foundation, La Habra, California. All rights reserved.

Scriptures marked ESV are from the Holy Bible, English Standard Version® (ESV®)
Copyright © 2001 by Crossway, a publishing ministry of Good News Publishers.
All rights reserved.

Scriptures marked NIV are from the New International Version.
Copyright 2011 by Biblica. All rights reserved.

Endorsement:

Kingdom Mentoring gave us a unique blend of foundational biblical teaching and powerful practical application in carrying the good news of Jesus to the world around us. Steven and Helen carry a wonderful blend of pastoral, apostolic and prophetic gifting, and many of our church members felt dangerously emboldened in their faith as a result of this course. A rich resource for believers everywhere, I highly commend this for anyone wanting to grow into their full identity in Christ.

Simon Dennis, Pastor, Sheddocksley Baptist Church, Aberdeen

OL

CW01501839

The purpose of this book, and the equipping courses that we run, is to develop mature disciples of Jesus Christ who are released effectively into the mission of the kingdom of God. We have many tutors or teachers but few fathers in the Lord (1 Corinthians 4:15). This is a course, not only for instruction and teaching, which it does include, but for the discipling of our hearts as we are connected to the heart of the Father. It is out of the Father's blessing our hearts will be healed, free, and secure, and from that foundation we will release the works of His kingdom on the earth. This is accessible to all believers in Jesus Christ.

For those new to the faith, we first recommend *Life to the Full* by Steven Anderson and James Renwick which provides a basic building block for life in following Jesus.

As you go through this book read slowly and take time to follow through the various responses at the end of each chapter. The material contained is in a concise form allowing you to explore further. You may do this on your own or with a group, or as part of one of our Kingdom Mentoring courses.

To contact us or to find out more about our courses and how to host one locally or online:

E-mail: stevenjohnanderson1@gmail.com or visit our Kingdom Mentoring Facebook page

INTRODUCTION

When I was 20 years old the Lord took hold of me in a way I did not understand. Something had gripped me, awakening a deeper longing within, drawing me out in a search for so much more than I knew or had experienced. This 'upward call' invited and challenged me into that which was beyond my present understanding. It was a call to 'seek first the kingdom of God,' yet it would be another four years before I would experience a powerful baptism in the Holy Spirit, seeing an unfolding of the meaning and demonstration of His kingdom. A new adventure had begun!

As this call began to clarify, two key Scriptures came forcibly to my attention:

Enlarge the place of your tent, stretch your tent curtains wide, do not hold back; lengthen your cords, strengthen your stakes. Isaiah 54:2 (NIV)

I pray that out of his glorious riches he may strengthen you with power through his Spirit in your inner being, so that Christ may dwell in your hearts through faith. And I pray that you, being rooted and established in love, may have power, together with all the

Lord's holy people, to grasp how wide and long and high and deep is the love of Christ, and to know this love that surpasses knowledge — that you may be filled to the measure of all the fullness of God. Ephesians 3:16-19 (NIV)

These verses speak to us of stretching and strengthening, of breaking through and building. If we stretch too far without strengthening, we can snap, if we gain great breakthrough but don't build on it, we will soon see what we gained fade and fall away.

The kingdom of God — His life-giving rule and realm — is continually breaking in to our realm, is increasing and will forever increase (Isaiah 6:7). God desires to stretch us and to strengthen us so we can stretch out even further. He calls us to break through into enemy held territories and to build His Kingdom there as we displace the domination of darkness.

This is an equipping manual for living a life of experiencing and expressing the kingdom of God here on earth. Building on the solid foundations provided in Christ and God's Word, and by growing in deepening relationship with God the Father, Son and Spirit, we mature and are led by Him into life-transforming and world-shaping expressions of prayer, prophecy, proclamation and power.

As we embark on this adventure make sure to build well, digging deep into the 'unsearchable riches of Christ Jesus,' and be ready to break out into new ground, taking hold of that for which He took hold of you.

INTRODUCTORY SECTION
EQUIPPING: PREPARING THE NETS

Going a little farther, He saw James the son of Zebedee, and John his brother, who were also in the boat mending the nets. Mark 1:19

Jesus is walking along the shores of the Sea of Galilee and calling, inviting and challenging certain fishermen to come and follow Him. Zebedee's sons are in their boat doing what any fishermen would do after one catch and before launching out for another. They are mending their nets. That is preparing them, repairing them, and making them fit for their intended purpose. After Jesus is raised from the dead, He appears to His disciples by the lake shore instructing them to cast their nets on the other side. They take in a large catch, yet it says that the nets did not break (John 21:11). They had been well mended and were ready for purpose. Likewise, the Lord is equipping us to be fit for purpose that we might bring in a large harvest.

We are in this kingdom adventure with others. A net cannot be formed from one strand, but we need to be linked and joined together. None of us can accomplish our fullest potential without the partnership of both the Holy Spirit and others in the Body of Christ. Paul prays in Ephesians 3:18 that we 'may be able to comprehend together with all the saints (God's people) what is the breadth and length and height and depth.'

There is an important word used in reference to the mending of the nets: *katartizo* which means to furnish completely, to complete, to equip and to prepare. The related word '*katartismos*' is found in Ephesians 4:12 referring to the role of the apostles, prophets, evangelists, shepherds and teachers – the Ascension gift ministries from Christ Jesus to His people – which are to equip God's people for works of service.

A FULLER MEANING OF EQUIP:
There are fuller meanings of these terms which we find from their use in other places. We will use the term 'equip' throughout, but by that we will include the ideas of renewing, restoring, refreshing, resourcing, and realigning. To equip then is much more than teaching or training but involves and affects the whole of our being.

Renewing The Lord brings a renewal of life to us, and especially a renewing of our minds (Romans 12:2) and a renewing of the very spirit of our mind (Ephesians 4:23), that is not just what we think but the whole manner in which we think.

Restoring Similarly, the Lord restores our life or our soul (Psalm 23:3). Father, Son and Holy Spirit created us according to their likeness (Genesis 1:26), and though that likeness was deformed by sin, we are now being restored as a new creation into the likeness of Jesus Christ (Romans 8:29).

Refreshing Times of refreshing come from the presence of the Lord (Acts 3:19) who makes all things new. The Lord refreshes us through the living water of His Spirit where we have become dry or weary, and He also refreshes us into our original purpose in Christ.

Resourcing The Lord is our provider in every way. Jesus is our source and from Him we keep receiving grace upon grace that continually re-sources us. He has qualified us and equips us with the gifts of His Spirit.

Realigning The Greek word was also used as a medical term for the realigning of broken bones. Likewise, the Lord realigns us to Himself and His will, and also realigns the broken or disjointed parts of His Body.

KEY WORDS ABOUT BIBLICAL EQUIPPING, DISCIPLING AND MENTORING:

Relational

_____

Developing

_____

Learning

_____

Experimenting

_____

Changing

_____

Reflecting

_____

Realising

_____

Discovering

_____

What do each of these words mean to you?

Which ones stand out most at this time of your life?

_____

_____

_____

_____

_____

The power of questions

Questions are a vital means for discovering. If we ask the wrong question, we will rarely get the right answer. If we ask the best questions then we will usually find the best answers. Throughout the Bible we see God asking people questions. These are very important questions that helped those individuals and groups discover something more of God's perspective and ways. For a study of 20 questions that are asked in the Old and New Testaments see my book _Discovery Questions_.

A great practice to develop is to both allow God to ask us questions and also to develop the skill of asking great questions. However, people do not often do this well which itself begs a question! Why don't people ask more questions?

1) They think they know what they need to know

2) They have no desire to learn and develop

3) They are too embarrassed

4) They don't know how or what to ask

Developing the practice of asking good questions
John Maxwell, in his book *Good Leaders Ask Great Questions* notes the following benefits of asking questions:
Questions unlock and open doors that otherwise remain closed
Questions connect people
Questions cultivate humility
Questions help you engage others in conversation
Questions allow us to build better ideas
Questions give us a different perspective
Questions challenge mindsets and get you out of ruts

Think about how you can develop a practice of asking great questions. Begin to write down questions that will help you explore and discover more of what God has for you.

_____

_____

_____

_____

_____

_____

_____

_____

_____

_____

_____

Cultivating for a harvest
Another Biblical image is of us being God's field (1 Corinthians 3:6-9), or cultivated land, from which He is preparing to produce a harvest. Paul speaks briefly here of planting and watering but the

cultivating process would include more. It might start with the breaking up of the soil or fallow ground (Hosea 10:12). So, in our hearts such ground is broken up and the weeds of previously held false understandings are unlearned and removed. The soil is now prepared, maybe fertilised, and readied to produce a harvest of 30, 60 and 100-fold. The new shoots are taken care of so that they fully develop, likewise we nurture and develop fresh understanding of the ways of God as He cultivates a life ready for abundant fruitfulness.

What is Jesus cultivating in your life at this time?

_____
_____
_____
_____

What do you want to see cultivated within you?

_____
_____
_____
_____

Equip: God provides through His Word and the ministries He gives to the Body several means of equipping. These are essentially about readying His people to reveal Jesus Christ.

Activate: We can get lots of equipping just as we can get lots of teaching and gain much knowledge. However, unless this is activated it will not produce the desired and designed fruitfulness. Prophetic words and the laying on of hands are two of the means of activating the gifts and equipping of the Spirit of God (1 Timothy 4:14).

Release: Finally, there needs to be permission given for mission. We must not hold the equipped believers into involvement only in the structures of church life or to serve other people's ministries, but loose them into the harvest field of the Lord (Matthew 9:38). There must be an avenue of release that provides the opportunities to operate with the Spirit to present Jesus and the power of His kingdom.

In his book *Scattered Servants* Alan Scott says, "Our calling and mission is to carry the kingdom beyond the church into the heart of culture. As sent people, the *core* of the church is no longer defined as those who support the structure of church, but those who are transforming culture as church. The 'core' are not those who give and serve to keep the church going and growing; the core are those who risk to release the kingdom."

The Main Themes of the Bible:
Two great themes of the Bible which help us to understand the ways of God are **Covenant** and **Kingdom**. God initiates and calls people into a covenant relationship with Himself, and out of that relationship He trains us to reign with Him in bringing forth His kingdom on earth. We are brought into a covenant union with a kingdom expression.

Covenant: What does the Bible mean by the term covenant? It was an agreement between two parties which had certain terms and a legal force. The most common covenant in modern life is that of marriage where two people make a binding agreement through the exchanging of vows expressing their lifelong support and commitment to one another. In the Old Testament there are several covenants that God makes with people such as Abraham, Moses and David, and with Israel. At the heart of these covenants is

God's desire to have a people for Himself and to whom He expresses His lovingkindness.

In Christ, God has now made a new covenant that supersedes all other covenants. God initiates the covenant, He alone sets its terms, it is founded solely by His grace, and is maintained and operates by grace. Jesus dealt with our sin problem so that we can live in covenant relationship with a holy God. Because this covenant is by grace, sealed by the blood of Jesus, our response must be one of faith. We cannot earn any rights to the covenant blessings but receive them by faith. Because this covenant is based on what Jesus has accomplished, we can live eternally secure in this covenant relationship. It is through covenant relationship that we find our new identity as His people, as sons and daughters of God.

Kingdom: The kingdom of God, or as it is often termed in Matthew's Gospel, the kingdom of heaven, is essentially the realm where the King rules and His will is done (Matthew 6:10). (Matthew, written to a primarily Jewish audience, tends to avoid using the name of God as this was seen as disrespectful among Jews, and hence mostly uses the term kingdom of heaven). Just as an earthly kingdom would be the geographical area that a king or queen rules over, so the kingdom of God is the realm on earth where the King of Kings has His rule. This was fully expressed in the life of Jesus; hence the good news of the kingdom and the good news of Jesus Christ are essentially the same.

Jesus' message clearly focussed on the kingdom of God (Mark 1:15) and His works of healing and miracles were demonstrations of the kingdom rule of God over sickness, demons, disease and death. It may also be expressed in the righting of wrongs; the releasing of oppression and bringing forth justice. Human efforts at this can often lead to a different form of oppression as only in Christ can we find the adequate means for true redemption.

Jesus brought or inaugurated the kingdom of God on the earth but its fulfilment is yet to come. The kingdom of God is both present and future, now and not yet, but we should not make that an excuse for seeing little evidence of the kingdom now where we are. The kingdom is always increasing and we should be seeking to bring in more of His kingdom reality every day.

We will explore the greater depths of this covenant relationship, or union with Christ, which we have been brought into by His sacrifice for us, and then the outworking of that as we partner with Him in the works of His kingdom.

KEY BELIEFS, VALUES AND PRACTICES

Ponder and think through the implications of each of these for your life. It is very important to establish foundational truth into our hearts that will lead us through all the various situations of life.

1. God is good, and His love endures forever

Jesus brings good news, in Him there is always a better word. God is always good – that's an absolute truth of Who He is. This truth is not changed by how we feel, by what happens to us or what is going on in the world. His love endures through every situation; through every joy and through every tragedy; through every success and through every failure. The song of God's people for millennia has been, 'Give thanks to the LORD, for He is good, and His love endures forever.' It is good to sing this often!

2. Be impressed with Jesus

And He will make His impression on you. As we take time to behold Jesus, to gaze upon Him in adoration, to focus on His life and works, to ponder His amazing sacrifice for us, to glory in the wonder of His resurrection, and to worship Him upon His throne, then we are changed; transformed from glory to glory (2 Corinthians 3:18). This is all a part of God's eternal purpose to conform us to the likeness of His Son (Romans 8:29).

3. A heart of integrity

The grace of God has found us out for who we really were and is now making us who we truly are in Christ, therefore we have nothing to hide, nothing to prove and nothing to fear. As we receive God's grace and love our heart or inner being is brought together from its broken, divided and disintegrating state. We are integrated in Him, that is made whole. Such an undivided heart can live in consistency and honesty, and need give no place to the stumbling-blocks of offence, hypocrisy or deceit.

4. Trust in the Lord and live generously

Generosity is at the heart of who God is and the expression of His goodness and grace. Because He is generous to us, we can always give and forgive. Generosity is the means to and the purpose of God's provision and prospering of our souls. As we trust in God to meet our every need, we can continue to freely give away, knowing that the riches of His grace and glory to us will never run dry.

5. Everything is possible to the one who believes

Jesus has won the ultimate victory so there is always hope, opportunity and possibility. Our one necessity is to believe – not just to believe about Jesus but to believe in Him. Faith is vital to connect us into the limitless possibilities of God. Unbelief is one of the great barriers to God's works, such that even Jesus was hindered by His home town's unbelief (Mark 6:1-6).

What could each of the above look like in your life?

_____

_____

_____

_____

_____

_____

_____

_____

_____

_____

What needs to happen and develop in you for this to come about?

_____

_____

_____

_____

_____

_____

_____

_____

PART 1: FULLY ALIVE TO GOD

Consider yourselves to be dead to sin, but alive to God in Christ Jesus

Romans 6:11

In this section we will explore our relationship with God who has revealed Himself as three persons – Father, Son and Holy Spirit. To develop a healthy life, the fullness of life that Jesus came to give us, it is vital that we grow in relationship with all three persons of the Godhead: that we know the Son, that through Him the Father is fully revealed to us, and from Him we receive the Holy Spirit in all His fulness.

In the covenant relationship we are loved with an everlasting love. Our response is to love the Lord with all our being, to love one another and to love our neighbour as ourselves. Of course, we soon realised that as we were we could not fulfil these requirements. God does not work with our old life to try and bring some self-improvement. No, He puts that life, that old self in Adam to death. We have been crucified with Christ and buried with Him (Romans 6:4) and have been made a new creation, a new person created in righteousness and holiness in Christ (2 Corinthians 5:17; Ephesians 4:24). This is so we can walk in newness of life (Romans 6:4) and to do that we must as Paul says in Romans 6:11, 'consider yourselves to be dead to sin.' *If we still see ourselves as sinners, we will have a sinner mentality which is predisposed to fall and fail. As we now consider ourselves alive to God, we can increasingly walk in this newness of life that Jesus gives us.*

Now we discover that we can love because He first loved us (1 John 4:19). We are no longer wearily struggling to live up to an unachievable standard, but allowing the love that God pours into our hearts to overflow back to Him and outward to other people.

To live in this newness of life we need to be fully awakened to and alive to God. This awakening to newness of life begins through the grace of the Lord Jesus Who reveals to us the love of the Father Who fills us with His Holy Spirit that we might walk in partnership with Him upon the earth.

Response

Key question

From what viewpoint are you seeing yourself?

Who are you considering yourself to be?

_____

_____

_____

_____

_____

_____

_____

1. THE FREEDOM OF GRACE

The covenant relationship we are brought into is established through a work of grace, the grace of the Lord Jesus Christ. Jesus completed His work on the cross and cried, "It is finished," that is fulfilled and complete. Nothing can or need be added! Paul declares, "For by grace you have been saved through faith; and that not of yourselves, it is the gift of God" (Ephesians 2:8).

What then is this grace? It is often described as the undeserved or unmerited favour of God. Our salvation, and our continuing newness of life, is dependent on what Jesus has accomplished on our behalf and is received by us by faith. We had a debt we could never repay. Jesus paid the debt out of the mercy of God. But more than that He supplies us with the endless riches of grace. Imagine someone owed a debt of £100,000 and had no means whatsoever to repay this. The one to whom they owe the money cancels the debt. Wow! Now that is mercy! The one who was in such debt is free from that burden but has no money and maybe no means of making money and might soon end up in debt once more. But if the one who cancelled the debt also kept making funds available to the ex-debtor, though totally undeserved, then that is grace.

We are saved by grace and now live in the grace of God. Grace is not just some theological concept, but the expression of God's goodness that He wants us to experience. Jesus comes 'full of grace and truth' and from His fullness we receive grace upon grace (John 1:14, 16). John continues saying, "the Law was given through

Moses; grace and truth were realised (literally 'came to be') through Jesus Christ" (John 1:17). As the New American Standard translation suggests this grace and truth needs to in some way be realised, that is understood, apprehended and come forth as a reality in our lives. Grace is to be experienced, but first needs to be known and understood. So, Paul speaks of the need to understand or come to fully know the grace of God in truth (Colossians 1:6). This is the foundation that enables us to live according to the riches of His grace (Ephesians 1:7; 2:7). These riches are unsearchable yet are to be explored and increasingly discovered. They are immeasurable and unfathomable (Ephesians 3:8) yet we are invited to partake, and we find that the more we receive the more we realise there is even more!

We are to live according to these riches of grace. Often people live according to their means, though some try to live beyond their means financially and end up in debt! We might live according to certain rules or principles, or according to the way life has seemed to treat us. In Christ we are invited into a new way of living which is always according to these unlimited riches of His grace. Yet we can struggle to grasp this as it can be so foreign to all we have known in life. We can be conditioned to believe that we get rewarded for good behaviour and punished for bad behaviour, so have an aim to change our bad behaviour to good. Yet that has often led to an endless cycle of failing or living in pretence. God doesn't demand a change in behaviour in itself, but through grace makes us a new person in Christ, gives us a new identity and then invites and challenges us to live according to who we now are while continually supplying grace that enables to do this.

GRACE FREES US FROM OUR NEED:
1. **Of pretence – we have nothing to hide.** We don't need to pretend to be what we are not, we don't have to pretend to be good, but just be God's. Grace frees us to be honest.

2. **To defend ourselves – what we build we must defend so it's always open to threat.** What we receive by grace, God defends thus removing the power of threat and fear.

When we realise that no-one can take away what we have by grace, then people cease to be a threat – we can view everyone differently. No-one has power to diminish you when your life is built on God's grace. The stumbling stone has become our cornerstone.

3. **To justify or make excuses for ourselves – Jesus found us in a position of guilt and justified us**. No amount of self-justifying can add to that – it's totally unnecessary.

The grace of Jesus Christ is so wonderful, liberating, and enabling!

Becoming fully alive to Jesus and the riches of His grace first required that we die! And that is what happened. We died to the old life rooted in Adam, got buried with Christ in baptism and rose with Him as a new creation. We have been baptised into Christ, into His life. Paul tells us that we "are all sons (male and female ones!) of God through faith in Christ Jesus. For all of you who were baptised into Christ have clothed yourselves with Christ" (Galatians 3:26-27). The new self who is raised up in Christ, receives the status of son and therefore heir. We can now let go of all of our supposed rights and receive and share in His inheritance. So, the apostles speak of themselves as bondslaves who have no rights of their own, but also as sons who belong in the family and have full rights to 'the riches of the glory of His inheritance' (Ephesians 1:18).

THE FUNDAMENTAL SHIFT

As we are baptised into Christ, a fundamental shift takes place within that requires the renewing of the spirit of our minds so we can live in the freedom and joy that this brings. This is a shift from law and works based salvation to grace; from rules to relationship; from being driven to being led; from a pre-occupation with what you lack, to a declaration of what you have; from reacting to initiating; from being influenced to influencing; from being controlled by circumstances to creating possibilities. We can know of this but easily bend back to the old ways unless there's a fundamental shift in us. That is a work of the Spirit of Christ that we experience in our inner being.

With that shift we can enter into the very experience of Jesus' own baptism. Luke recounts that when Jesus was baptised 'the heaven was opened, and the Holy Spirit descended upon Him in bodily form like a dove, and a voice came out of heaven. "You are My beloved Son; in you I am well-pleased"' (Luke 3:21-22). Therefore, in Christ we can receive and enter into all of the following:

Access to the heavenly realm: As Jesus prayed the heavens were opened and they haven't closed back over. Jesus has opened the way, giving us access to the throne of grace and into the unseen heavenly realm that surrounds us.

Abiding of the Spirit: In the Old Testament the Spirit of God would come upon someone for a task and lift off again. Jesus, John the Baptist was told, was the One on whom the Spirit would come and remain (John 1:33). He then baptises us with the Holy Spirit who remains or abides with us forever.

Anointing of the Spirit: The Spirit not only abides but also anoints us to do the works of the kingdom of God. Jesus quotes Isaiah 61 saying that the Spirit of the Lord was upon Him, having anointed Him to preach the good news, proclaiming release and freedom for the oppressed (Luke 4:18). For the same purposes the anointing oil of the Spirit is poured upon us.

Affirmation of the Father: The voice of the Father speaks from heaven affirming and declaring who Jesus is – His beloved Son. He declares His pleasure with Jesus, though this was prior to any of Jesus' public ministry and works. The Father speaks this affirmation over us who are in Christ, not because of what we have done or achieved but simply for who we are as sons.

Affection of the Father: The Father's words are powerfully affirming and also display His affection towards Jesus and us. We are His beloved, a term the apostle John reminds us of as he speaks of the Father's love (see 1 John 3:1-2). The love of the Father is in no way cold or distant but deeply affectionate as He delights in us.

Adoption into Sonship: In Christ we receive this full rights adoption into the family forever. We are redeemed that we might receive adoption into sonship and the Spirit of His Son into our hearts (Galatians 4:5, 6). Paul elsewhere contrasts this spirit of adoption with the spirit of slavery to fear which we have all known in some way. Now the Spirit testifies with our spirit that we are God's children (Romans 8:15-16). It's a done deal and sealed forever.

Authority of Sonship: This sonship has great privilege and great responsibility. We are to represent the Father on earth and are given authority to release the will of heaven upon the earth. From His baptismal experience, Jesus, filled with the Spirit is tested on this very issue: 'if you are the Son of God...' and overcoming returns in the power of the Spirit and begins to exercise His authority over all darkness (Luke 4:1-14).

We who are baptised into Christ Jesus receive all this in Him. We too will be tested and tried, and indeed we will suffer with Him that we might also be glorified with Him (Romans 8:17). And so, Jesus brings us to the Father and reveals the Father to us, saying that 'no one knows the Son except the Father; nor does anyone know the Father except the Son, and anyone to whom the Son wills to reveal Him' (Matthew 11:27).

God the Father of our Lord Jesus Christ

Jesus came to be the Way to the Father (John 14:6); He reveals God as Father, His Father.

We can only know the Father as Jesus reveals Him to us. He does this through His relationship with His Father – it is relational revelation. We can likewise only know Jesus as the Son as the Father reveals Him. This also is in the dynamic of their relationship. Only a son can reveal a father and Jesus shows us how to relate as a son to God as Father. This revelation of the Father gives us understanding of our sonship and how to relate to God as 'sons' – to relate to Father as Jesus related to Him.

In this relationship with the Father, the Spirit also comes to release in us the language of children of God who cry out, "Abba, Father" (Romans 8:15; Galatians 4:6). This represents our lifelong dependence, love-based obedience, and deep security that we find in this Father-son relationship. As we cry out with the Spirit every part of our life and being comes alive to a recognition of who God is as our Abba, Father. This is not just something we read only, but something we must do, expressing the revelation that the Spirit brings and entering into the experience of the Father's love.

Response
Checklist: Evidence of the fundamental shift
What do you observe in the way you live and the manner of your thinking?

Slip back into Law and works based salvation or walk in the freedom of God's grace?

Wanting to know the rules or enjoying the relationship?

Being driven by demands or being led by the Spirit of God?

Being pre-occupied with what you think you lack or declaring of what you have in Christ?

Reacting to people and circumstances or initiating opportunities?

Being influenced by the world around you or influencing your world from the influence of heaven?

Being controlled by circumstances or creating possibilities?

2. THE FATHER'S BLESSING

The grace of Jesus Christ enables us to be brought into full relationship with His Father and our Father. The God we worship is the Father of our Lord Jesus Christ, and only Jesus the Son can connect us into covenant union with God.

As we live in the dynamic of relationship with God the Father, God the Son and God the Spirit two confessions come to our lips – Jesus is Lord and Abba, Father. Both of these are enabled by the Holy Spirit (1 Corinthians 12:3; Galatians 4:6). We are invited into the relationships of the Godhead. This is all more than we can fully comprehend and much more than theory written in books. This is a living experience, truly living a life to the full that we are continually invited and challenged to come further into. Jesus reveals God as Father and the Spirit brings the realisation into our being.

As we receive this revelation of God as Father, we can hit up against two main obstacles. The first is where we have had a very different view of God than that of the loving Father of Jesus. If deep down we have accepted a view of God primarily as a stern, austere judge, or a distant deity then some thinking needs to be undone from the spirit of our minds. Though there is truth in that God is Judge, yet Jesus' primary and clear presentation of Him is as Father.

The second obstacle can be in our ideas and feelings around the term 'father.' There has been a wide range of experience of earthly fathers from good and loving to absent and abusive. None are perfect and some are a million miles from perfect. For some there may need to be both a mental uprooting of wrong images and a healing of wounded areas of the soul. There may be some specific memories that need healed but also healing comes as we receive by faith the revelation from Jesus of the Father.

Jesus has prayed a wonderful prayer that we find in John 17. At the end of this He prays concerning how He has made the Father's name (that is His true nature) known to us, and how He will continue to make it known so that the love with which the Father has loved Jesus may be in us (John 17:26). Wow! That is Jesus' prayer that the love with which the Father loved Him would be known to us. That is the will of God and will be fulfilled. As we receive this now, we can live in the experiential knowledge of His love and the amazing freedom that brings to us in so many ways.

We can almost hear the apostle John shout out as he writes, "See how great a love the Father has bestowed on us" (1 John 3:1). The Father's love and blessing is the desire of all creation even if many people do not yet recognise this. Paul says that, "the anxious longing of the creation waits eagerly for the revealing of the sons of God" (Romans 8:19), that there would be a great revelation of the Father and His love through many sons. As Mark Stibbe says in his book, *I am Your Father*, "in a cold and fallen cosmos, we are all of us spiritual orphans, trying to find our way home into the true Father's arms." Thank God that Jesus is the way, has made the way and shows us the way.

The great need for us as believers is to truly know the Father's love that meets our every need for security and significance, that we would serve God's purposes, not to gain His favour but from having received His favour. We have nothing to prove, no need to try and gain something over someone else, no place for competition or comparison, because we already are loved with an everlasting love. It is this love that brings wholeness and forms integrity in our hearts. There is such beauty in living and serving out of the unquenchable love of our Father and this eliminates the ugliness of performance based and point scoring works.

There is a great need too in our world for a revelation of the Father's love to conquer the growing pandemic levels of fatherlessness across the nations. Over the years of ministering in several nations and in prisons or among many broken people, we have seen the sad evidence of the lack of fathering and the damage caused by broken fathering. Again, Stibbe writes, "the whole planet is waiting for Christian believers to rise up as the adopted sons and daughters of *Abba*, Father." Then we can show the Father and release His healing love into countless hearts.

THE EFFECT OF THE FATHER'S LOVE

John states that "we love, because He first loved us" (1 John 4:19). Freely we must receive so we can freely give. We must allow the Holy Spirit to impart this love to us, "because the love of God has been poured out within our hearts through the Holy Spirit" (Romans 5:5). We need to let Him uproot wrong understandings, penetrating our inner being, passed any fear-based defences, and heal our damaged memories. This perfect love will indeed drive out all fear (1 John 4:18). As part of Adam's race, we have all been born with a primal root of fear. This is managed in many people's lives but can be debilitating and devastating in others.

The basis of this fear is separation from God. John says fear has to do with punishment and the ultimate punishment is separation from God. It is the separation that sin brings that enables fear to run amok throughout the human race. Once we come into covenant union with Christ then, as Paul states, "(nothing) will be able to separate us from the love of God, which is in Christ Jesus" (Romans 8:39). The very basis of fear has been removed!

With the removing of a fear-based existence we are drawn into a love-based life. Here we find wholeness as we are now rooted and established in the love of God. Tom Smail in his excellent book *The Forgotten Father* writes, "a father means somebody who is able to regulate the life of his children from a centre outside themselves, to pull them towards wholeness, to accustom them to obedience and so to offer them security." A fear-based life necessarily looks out for itself, to protect itself, and is ultimately self-centred. The Father's love shows us that we are not the centre of the universe, nor need to be, and draws us out into a life of trusting obedience to Him. In trusting and submitting our life to the authority of God we find the place of greatest security. In obeying the Father, we find a life of the greatest significance.

THE FATHER'S BLESSING

The greatest desire of every human heart is to know the Father's blessing. The first thing God did when He created man (male and female) was to bless them (Genesis1:27-28). Sin and disobedience have stolen away the blessing, but our hearts all still long for it.

To bless means to affirm, nurture, call to full life, want and speak good towards, to give permission, and to empower to prosper, thrive and be fruitful. Who doesn't want that? We have all sought this, first from our parents, and then from significant other people in our lives. Some have found and received a measure of this blessing while others have searched largely in vain. Ultimately, we all lack the fullness of this until we receive it from the voice of the true Father as Jesus did: "This is My beloved Son, with Whom I am well-pleased."

The Father's blessing brings a powerful spiritual impartation into our lives that releases healing to our inmost being and sets in motion a great redemptive work. His words of blessing break the power of previously received words of curse and restriction. His blessing takes the small bud of our soul and calls it into full flower, flourishing and fruitfulness. As God blessed them in the garden at the beginning, He then commissioned them to be fruitful and multiply. Likewise, Jesus' very last act before ascending to heaven was to bless His disciples (Luke 24:50-51) as He was commissioning them to go into all the world bearing the fruit of the good news of the kingdom and multiplying themselves everywhere. We are blessed to be a blessing.

MATURING SONS

As we receive the Father's love and blessing, we are enabled to grow up as mature sons and daughters. In Jesus' Sonship we find ours, and in this we find freedom. "If the Son makes you free, you will be free indeed" (John 8:36). The entanglements of religious rules and of works-based salvation have been loosed; there are no 'add-ons' to the grace of Christ Jesus. Now we can use this freedom in different ways but as we walk in trusting, dependant obedience to the Father we will grow up in all things into maturity and the fullness of Christ (Ephesians 4:13). The world is desperate to see the maturing sons and daughters of God whose every cell knows and cries out, 'Abba, Father!'

Response:

Through the grace of Jesus Christ come before the Father. You have nothing to hide – you're forgiven; you have nothing to prove – Jesus has qualified you; you have nothing to fear – you are accepted in the Beloved.

Receive His acceptance, affirmation, and approval: You are His beloved son/daughter; with you He is well-pleased. Hear those words over and over and let them sink deep into your inner being.

Listen for His words of blessing to you.

Release your expressions of love, adoration, thanks, and worship back to Him as your spirit cries out, 'Abba, Father!'

3. PARTNERSHIP AND POWER

We are in covenant relationship with God the Father, Son and Holy Spirit. It is vital for our maturing in our sonship that we can relate in a healthy manner to each of the persons of the Godhead. Paul prays a blessing upon the church at Corinth that the grace of the Lord Jesus Christ, the love of God and fellowship of the Holy Spirit would be with them (2 Corinthians 13:14). Having looked at the grace of Christ and the love of God the Father we now turn to our relationship with the Person of the Holy Spirit.

Paul speaks of the 'fellowship' of the Holy Spirit. The Greek word *koinonia* translates also as partnership or association, and comes from a root meaning, 'to have in common.' We receive the Holy Spirit, the promise of the Father through Jesus, and He comes and abides in us. We have a growing, deepening personal relationship with Him which manifests in several ways. We walk with the Spirit, in step with Him, in a partnership where we share the common purpose of testifying to Jesus and glorifying Him (John 15:26; 16:14).

However, it can be challenging to grow in this relationship as the Spirit is like the wind which blows wherever it wills and is hard if not impossible to catch. He is the breath of God, at times mysterious and hard to comprehend, and He is like streams of living water flowing from within us, waters that cannot be contained. The Holy Spirit has been associated at times with some bizarre expressions and at other times relegated from His true place in the life of the church. But it is abundantly clear from Scripture that the Holy Spirit is an equal Person of the Godhead, and that His presence and power were vital in the life and ministry of Jesus, and are of course equally vital in our lives and ministries.

Jesus laid aside His glory and came to earth as fully man, not some half-god, half-man combination. He did not do miracles because He was God (and He always was and is fully God) but as a man, the true Son of Man who was in perfect relationship with His Father and filled with the Holy Spirit. Jesus began His public ministry after His baptism where He was filled with the Holy Spirit, then after being tested, returned in the power of the Holy Spirit (Luke 4:1, 14). He has now created the same playing field for us – He has made us righteous before God through His blood, and He baptises us in the Holy Spirit. This is the basis from which we go forward in the works of the kingdom of God.

The promise was that as John the Baptist baptised people in water, the Coming One, Jesus, would baptise in and with the Holy Spirit (John 1:33). Jesus Himself told His disciples after He had risen from the dead that they would be baptised with the Holy Spirit not many days from then (Acts 1:5), which was fulfilled on the day of Pentecost. Indeed, Peter recalls at one point, 'how He (Jesus) used to say, "John baptised with water, but you will be baptised with the Holy Spirit"' (Acts 11:16). The verb used suggests that Jesus said this on a number of occasions – it was something He emphasised as of great importance. The early believers also emphasised this, seeking to ensure that all new believers received a demonstrable filling of the Spirit (Acts 8:14-17; 19:1-6).

When we are born anew of the Spirit, we are to be baptised in and with Him, and then be continually filled with Him. In Ephesians 5:18 Paul instructs us to be continually filled with the Spirit (which he contrasts with being drunk on wine!), which is an invitation to an endless receiving of the immeasurable. Interestingly, the early believers at Pentecost were thought by some to be filled with new wine, suggesting that sometimes the outward manifestation of the Holy Spirit may resemble being intoxicated but with something infinitely better and life-giving!

When I came to faith in Jesus and was truly born anew of the Spirit, I did not understand the meaning of being baptised in the Holy Spirit. It wasn't taught or expected, yet there was a growing sense within me that God had something more for me. I went on a journey for a time which culminated at a conference in Brighton, England where I had hands laid on me for this Spirit baptism. Initially I felt nothing really, but an hour or so later I found myself praying in a new language of tongues. More than that I felt a huge shift within, and on returning home my wife, Helen, saw that a very different Steven had returned from Brighton than the one who went.

The early believers were all filled with the Holy Spirit in the upper room, and were filled again a little later such that the building shook (Acts 4:31). Our need is to be baptised, filled and move in the power of the Spirit. So, let's look at what He brings to us as we are baptised and filled with Him:

THE ANOINTING OF THE SPIRIT (Luke 4:18; Acts 10:38)

The Old Testament speaks of the anointing oil that was smeared onto the head of the priests as they were ordained and consecrated (Exodus 28:41). The anointing came to mean the alighting of the Spirit of God for a task as we see in Luke 4:18, "The Spirit of the Lord is upon Me, because He has anointed Me to preach good news." Even when we are filled with the Spirit there is still more of Him to come, and so He may come on us in a specific manner to anoint us for a particular task or at a particular moment. Acts 10:38 says that God anointed Jesus and He went about doing good and healing. When God calls us to specific works and ministries, we can expect His anointing for the task.

THE POWER OF THE SPIRIT (Luke 4:14; Acts 1:8)

We also see in Acts 10:38 that Jesus was anointed with the Holy Spirit and with power. In Luke 4:1 we find Jesus described as being full of the Holy Spirit, but after He returns from overcoming the evil one, He is now described as being in the power of the Spirit (Luke 4:14). It seems we can be filled with the Spirit but not dynamically moving in His power. We need both, and like Jesus the latter may come forth as we overcome in some areas. It is clearly the power of the Spirit that we need to move in as this is Jesus' promise in Acts 1:8 that we will receive power when the Holy Spirit comes upon us. This is power to be His witnesses, that is its primary purpose.

THE GIFTS OF THE SPIRIT (1 Corinthians 12:4-11)

The Holy Spirit is the Gift from the Father, it is Him we need. In turn He then distributes His gifts among us for the common good of building the church and making the good news visible and known. A key passage is 1 Corinthians 12 where Paul describes a gathering of believers. In that setting the Spirit moves, hovering over His people, and distributes manifestations or gifts to each one as required for His purposes at that time. He doesn't give one person a gift that is then 'their gift' in any possessive way. He gives the gift needed at that time. One time a person may receive the word of knowledge but another time the same person may receive a gift of healing for someone. As the Spirit fills us, we can all operate with any and all of His gifts as He wills. Paul's encouragement to us is to eagerly desire these gifts (1 Corinthians 14:1).

THE LANGUAGE OF THE SPIRIT (Acts 2:1-21)

While the Spirit empowers us to release healing, signs and wonders, one of His main roles is to bring revelation from heaven to earth.

On the day of Pentecost, He distributed tongues upon the believers enabling them to be heard declaring God's mighty works in various languages. Peter explains something of what is happening by quoting from the prophet Joel in vs 17-21. The emphasis is on all – sons and daughters, young and old, male and female – receiving the ability to prophesy, and to see and hear in the Spirit. The Spirit brings revelation and understanding, and the language to express it adequately.

THE FRUIT OF THE SPIRIT (Galatians 5:22-23)

Sometime people ask which is more important – the gifts or the fruit. That is simply the wrong question to ask, as God graciously and generously gives both. The fruit is not something we manufacture but the outworking of the Spirit's presence in our lives. He brings out the love of the Father, fills us with joy in His presence, establishes the peace of Christ in our hearts and more. Our aim should not be to strive hard to be more patient or kinder, but seek to be more completely filled with the Holy Spirit allowing His life and nature to ooze in and through us.

Response:
Fruit – language – gifts – power – anointing

They are all available to you

What are you experiencing?

What do you want to ask for?

Read Luke 11:13 and ask the Father on this basis

PART 2: A HOUSE OF PRAYER

*And Jesus entered the temple and drove out all those who were buying and selling in the temple, and overturned the tables of the money changers and the seats of those who were selling doves. And He said to them, "It is written, **'MY HOUSE SHALL BE CALLED A HOUSE OF PRAYER'** but you are making it a robbers' den.*
And the blind and the lame came to Him in the temple, and He healed them...And the children were shouting, "Hosanna to the Son of David."
Matthew 21:12-15

This House of Prayer is not a building but you and me; we are a temple of God in which His Spirit dwells (1 Corinthians 3:15). Wherever we are is a house of prayer. What we build in the hidden place with God will carry into the public place of worshipping and praying together with God's people.

Jesus cleanses temples and makes them houses of prayer where the blind and the lame are healed, and child-like hearts shout aloud their songs of praise. Here we make our first response to the revelation of the relationship we have in the grace of Jesus Christ, the love of the Father and the partnership with the Holy Spirit. We cry out as children of God: 'Abba, Father!' We declare as believers, 'Jesus is Lord!' We respond with thanksgiving, expressions of our love and delight in the Lord, and engage with the Holy Spirit in releasing God's will on earth as it is in heaven.

In Psalm 27:4 King David expresses his heart's true desire:

One thing I have asked from the LORD, that I shall seek:
That I may dwell in the house of the LORD All the days of my life,
To behold the beauty of the LORD
And the meditate (inquire) in His temple.

This is David's **one thing**, his priority and main focus. He is not some mystical character with little else to do, he is the king of a nation with its government on his shoulders. However, he had understood something of the utmost importance. He had observed the favour that came from the presence of God, so he established a tabernacle in Jerusalem to host the Ark of God's presence and respond in continual praise and prayer.

David **asked** for this; he desired to dwell in the Lord's house and he continued to **seek after** this. Many may ask but not so many truly seek until they find. His desire was to remain, abide and sit down resting in the Lord's presence.

There were then two main activities that flow from this place of restful abiding.

First to **behold the beauty of the Lord**, that is to see Him, to gaze upon the full revelation of His nature, being enthralled with His delightfulness. The word 'behold' can mean to see in the sense of a Seer who engages in the prophetic realm. Then, and only then, follows the second activity, that is to **inquire** in the presence of God. This word may be translated meditate and has the sense of searching, considering, sitting with and pondering. A time to bring our questions before the Lord, to seek His direction and understanding. This takes time, it is the fruit of relationship. Today we have search engines that produce thousands of results in seconds that put vast amounts of information at our fingertips. But that doesn't bring the transformation of the heart or the likeness of Jesus Christ. God speaks in various indistinct ways, and at times is quite silent, in order to draw us in to taking time in His presence.

As we respond to Him in expressions of worship; as we listen for His voice; as we partner with the Spirit in intercessory prayer we need to be in no rush. There is no set formula for success; there is no quick fix. But there is fruit of growing intimacy of relationship that is life-transforming and world-changing.

4. EXPRESSING DELIGHT

We praise God for Who He is and we thank Him for what he does. We behold His beauty and respond in an outbreak and overflow of our hearts in adoration. We enter His gates with thanksgiving and His courts with praise, then we proceed to the most Holy Place of His presence opened to us by the blood of the Lamb.

THE PURPOSE AND POWER OF PRAISE
Praise is fitting:

> *Sing for joy in the LORD, O you righteous ones;*
> *Praise is becoming to the upright.* Psalm 33:1

Remember we are made righteous and upright in Christ so this is speaking to us. Praise, the Psalmist says, is 'becoming,' that is befitting, well-suited and beautiful. It is just right and sits perfectly on us. God doesn't need or require our praise for His own sake, but invites us into an expression that stands us rightly in His presence and gives us a truer perspective on all of life. Praise acknowledges Who God truly is and gives us language of response.

Once we were cruising in the Norwegian fjords. As we sailed round into a fjord the magnificent scenery of the landscape came into view. Majestic mountains reflected in the still waters, and gushing waterfalls poured forth causing us both to gasp in amazement. How much more as we catch a glimpse of the Majesty of the Holy One will we gasp in wonder? And that gasp can turn to words and songs and various expressions as we are schooled by the Word and the Spirit.

Praise is life-renewing:

Isaiah 61:3 says that we are given, "the mantle of praise instead of the spirit of fainting." That's a great exchange! We can all experience the fainting spirit, and especially when we come to prayer. We can get distracted, discouraged, and sometimes just plain sleepy! The disciples of Jesus knew this on more than one occasion (Luke 9:32; 22:45-46). Praise is the antidote. It lifts our focus, stirs our spirit, moves our physical being, and engages our emotions in a positive and helpful way. We have been supplied with this mantle but we need to put it on. We may need to remind and rouse ourselves to praise as David did, calling our soul to praise and bless the Lord, and stirring all that is within us to do so (Psalm 103:1).

Praise is powerful:
Dismantling prisons – Acts 16:25-26

Paul and Silas were in a dark dungeon of a prison in Philippi. Rather than indulging in any self-pity or criticising those who opposed them these two men engage in prayer and sing songs of praise to God. It's midnight, it's very dark but as they lift their voices the prison shakes. First the foundations quake, then the doors fly open, and finally everyone's chains fall off! Praise has within it the power to dismantle enemy strongholds. And as we set people free it is important to first remove any foundation the enemy had, then open the door to the Lord, and as He enters chains fall off.

Constricting the enemy's activity – Psalm 149:5-9

The songs of praise from the saints of the Most High have a crushing effect upon Satan's activities. The enemy is greatly confined in an atmosphere of praise. The high praises of God act as a double-edged sword, and bind the work of demonic spirits.

Various Expressions of Praise: Psalm 105:1-5

Many of the Psalms issue a call to praise and encourage various expressions. Here in this Psalm, we find a helpful list:

(a) Give thanks (v1a) – this is a common exhortation throughout the Psalms and other Scriptures, e.g., Isaiah 12:4; Psalms 106:1; 107:1.

(b) Call upon His name (v1b) – once again a regular encouragement and practice in Scripture. David says in Psalm 18:3, "I will call upon the LORD, who is worthy to be praised, and I am saved from my enemies."

(c) Sing to Him (v2a) – a most common expression of praise in Old and New Testaments. It is a constant activity of heaven where the hosts sing a new song (Revelation 5:9).

(d) Speak of His wonders (v2b) – testifying to the wondrous works of God gives Him the honour due to Him and encourages praise in those who hear. As the Spirit fell on the believers at Pentecost this is exactly what they did in various tongues.

(e) Glory or boast in His holy name (v3a) – we have nothing in ourselves to boast of, but as Paul says more than once, "Let him who boasts, boast in the Lord." As we give glory we prepare for the day when the whole earth will be filled with the knowledge of the glory of the Lord.

(f) Be glad (v3b) – expressing gladness and joy is a much-needed expression of praise in response to the lavish riches of God's grace to us. We are called to sing and shout for joy and to rejoice. As we rightly rejoice in the Lord so His joy floods our hearts.

(g) Seek the Lord: His strength (v4a) and His face (v4b) – the very act of seeking Him, both His face and the fruit of His favour, honours Him.

(h) Remember His wonders (v5) – acts of remembering are important to us and Jesus gave us a very specific act of remembering in the Lord's Supper. We can easily grow dull in our appreciation of what the Lord has done and need regular acts of remembrance.

Our whole response to God is motivated by His grace, not forced by feelings of guilt. It is not some dry duty but a joy. He gives us joy in the house of prayer (Isaiah 56:7). We delight in Him who delights in us! Within this there is a place for developing devotional expressions of our adoration. There is a place for training our senses through spiritual disciplines that do not limit, but rather enhance the liberty we have in the Spirit of the Lord.

The Spirit brings revelation of who the Lord is to us in all His fullness. We don't get it all at first but must set ourselves to gaining greater understanding. This in turn moves us to respond but we don't always have the language to do so. The Spirit of God and the Word of God supply us with language to express our adoration. We will look at a few ways in which we can develop this practice and language of prayer and praise.

Beholding the Lord
2 Corinthians 3:18; Psalm 27:4
This was David's great desire and it is a necessary practice that leads to our being transformed into the likeness of Christ as we are moved from glory to glory. It is another way of saying one of our key practices: be impressed with Jesus and He will make His impression on you. Yet how do we do this?
First, we recognise that it is possible. The veil has been removed and we are invited into the most holy place. This is not some lofty spiritual exercise for the few but open to all who believe.
Second, make use of the Word of God and the descriptions of the risen Lord that it contains. Revelation 1:12-18 is great place to start.

Third, know that the Holy Spirit aids you in this. He seeks to glorify Jesus and 'will take of Mine,' says Jesus, 'and will disclose it to you.' He brings everything of Jesus to us, and through His wisdom and revelation brings us to a knowledge of Him.

Fourth, develop a practice over time. We don't immediately see clearly, but see dimly. The term 'as in a mirror' which Paul uses was not the sort of mirror we have today, but one that did not give a clear reflection (1 Corinthians 13:12). Be deliberate; set time; partner with the Spirit and the Word; wait in His presence, and begin to express adoration for even the dim beholding you have.

Meditating on the Word

Psalm 1:2; Colossians 3:16

Joshua was instructed to meditate on the book of the law both day and night. How much more so us who have the full Old and New Testaments. We are to read the word, study it, and obey it. One of the most helpful ways of letting the word 'dwell richly in us' is to meditate on it. The word 'meditate' means to consider, ponder, chew over, to mutter and to muse. This practice becomes a delight to us as the Psalmist states in Psalm 1:2. But how do we do it?

A simple practice I learned and have developed is this: **read it, write it, say it, sing and pray it!** Read the word, just a verse or a phrase at a time, and do this aloud. Faith comes by hearing the word, and this way it enters our eyes and our ears.

Write it down in a journal or somewhere else. Writing it out helps us retain it in our memory. Now say it, speaking it aloud once more as you begin to memorise it. Make it a declaration of truth. Now the interesting one, sing it! Yes, even if you have a tuneless tone, turn it into a little song. Get over any sense of embarrassment and give it a go. Singing does two things. Again, it aids memory as we remember so much more of what we sing then what we say. Also singing seems to activate something in the soul that can bring out a deeper appreciation and insight into the text. Finally, turn it into a prayer.

Calling on God's Covenant Names
We already noted that to call on the Lord was an expression of praise given in Psalm 105. More specifically we can call on the covenant names of God and take hold of the promises contained within them. God has revealed Himself throughout Scripture as a God of covenant. On particular occasions He revealed an aspect of His covenantal activity towards His people.

Here is a list of seven key covenant names of God which are all fulfilled and encompassed in Christ Jesus:
The LORD our Righteousness – Jeremiah 23:6
The LORD our Sanctifier – Exodus 31:13
The LORD our Provider – Genesis 22:14
The LORD our Banner – Exodos 17:15
The LORD our Peace – Judges 6:24
The LORD our Shepherd – Psalm 23:1
The LORD our Healer – Exodus 15:26

Singing the songs of Revelation
It is a great practice to develop singing the songs that are being sung in heaven. Here is a list of seven of these:
4:8 Holy, holy, holy!
4:11 You are worthy...For You created
5:9-10 You are worthy...For You were slain
5:12 Worthy is the Lamb
5:13; 7:12 Blessing and honour
15:3-4 Great and marvellous are Your works
19:6-7 The Lord God omnipotent reigns!

Praying the New Testament Prayers
Sometimes we don't know what to pray. The Spirit helps us in our weakness and the Scripture gives us insight into the prayers the apostles prayed. Again, here is a list of seven of these prayers which can be prayed one a day throughout the week:
Ephesians 1:17-19; 3:16-19; Romans 15:13; Colossians 1:9-12; Philippians 1:9-11; Acts 4:29-39; 2 Thessalonians 2:16-17.

Using the Psalms to express our hearts
There is an honesty in the Psalms that gives permission to express your feelings of struggle and at times dismay at what is going on in your life. The Psalms can give us good language to express the emotional turbulence we can experience on occasion. Psalm 13 is a great example which begins with various, 'how long?' questions in vs 1-2. It expresses a sense of frustration and wondering why God doesn't appear to help. It moves into an appeal in vs 3-4 before working through to a place of fresh trust expressed in vs 5-6.

Singing in the Spirit (the gift of tongues)
In 1 Corinthians 14:15 Paul is working through the place of tongues in worship. He concludes that he will both pray and sing with the spirit and with his mind. There is of course a great place to pray and praise God intelligently, with our understanding. But ultimately the Person of God and some of the ways and works of God are beyond our present understanding. We can reach a point where we seem to have exhausted all our own words. This is where the Spirit of God gives us the beautiful gifts of tongues, a heavenly language that takes us beyond, where we may not know what we are saying or singing, but our spirit soars in worship. We can ask for and receive an increase in the gifts of tongues and a release into song if we have never done this before.

An act of adoration: John 12:1-3

Jesus was at the home of Lazarus, who He had recently brought back from the grave. In response to being extremely impressed with Jesus, we see Mary pour out an act of deep adoration. It seems like she can't contain herself and she isn't worried about what anyone else thinks. She just goes for it. What do we notice about this act of adoration? First, it was very costly and therefore this appeared, and indeed was, a most extravagant act. Second, it was misunderstood and criticised especially by those who did not have such an appreciation for the Person of Jesus. Despite the opposing voices, this act of adoration filled the whole house with its fragrance.

Praying as a bride not as a widow

As we move from praise into prayer it is vital that we approach God out of who we are in relationship to Jesus. We can't be His widow because He is risen from the dead! We are His bride awaiting the marriage feast. There is a parable in Luke 18:1-8 which Jesus tells so that we would continue in steadfast prayer and not lose heart or grow faint. Praise is the antidote to the fainting spirit. This parable has often been misunderstood or only partially understood.

Basically, in this story a widow gets her answer for justice from an unrighteous judge because she pesters the life out of him. This is a parable of contrasts. Of course, we realise God is not an unrighteous judge but a good Father. However, we often stop there and still view ourselves or the church as the widow. If we have a widow mentality we will come begging, complaining, and seeking to wear God down. No! God the Father is the contrast to the judge in the parable, and the bride of Christ is the contrast to the widow. The parable is saying that if a widow can get justice from an unrighteous judge just by persisting, then how much more will the Father bring about justice for the bride of His Son.

Response

Remind yourself of how God sees you in Christ and of all He has done for you.
Release an expression of praise that you haven't used before.

Begin to develop a life of devoted adoration by using some of the practices outlined in this chapter. For example, start singing a song from the book of Revelation each day, and/or pray one of the New Testament prayers of the apostles every day.

Set aside a time, maybe one hour, to behold the Lord in His beauty. Start with praise, maybe using a worship song on a device, then read Revelation 1:12-18 and ask the Spirit to help you behold the Lord in your heart. Press in and write down what you sensed afterwards. Don't give up as even a few minutes of beholding Him has a transformational impact. Above all it pleases the Lord.

5. PROPHECY AND HEARING THE VOICE OF GOD

The day of Pentecost witnessed a wonderful fulfilment of Old Testament promise. Peter, as he preaches to the crowds, clearly links the happenings of that day to the prophet Joel's words from centuries beforehand (Joel 2:28-32; Acts 2:16-20). A major emphasis of those words from Joel was that as God poured out His Spirit there would be a great release of prophecy alongside dreams and visions. God would communicate in a more widespread way to His people with sons and daughters, old and young, men and women all prophesying.

Paul, while encouraging the seeking of the gifts of the Spirit, gives special attention to the earnest desire to prophesy (1 Corinthians 14:1). While there are new covenant prophets, who coupled with apostles build foundations in the church, the clear teaching of the Scriptures is that now all can prophesy. Indeed, a main role of prophets is to equip God's people to prophesy.

Jesus says that the sheep hear His voice (John 10:3) as He modelled a life of listening to and hearing the voice of His Father (John 8:28). He encouraged His disciples that the Holy Spirit would come guiding, speaking, disclosing and revealing the things of Christ to them (John 16:12-15).

God speaks today! He does so primarily through His Word, the bedrock of faith that is the Old and New Testaments. Yet, as these very Scriptures teach us, He speaks in various other means which align with the full revelation of His Son and never contradict what is written in His Word.

What is prophecy and why is it important in the house of prayer? How does God speak to us today and how does that guide us in intercessory prayer for His will to be done on earth as it is in heaven?

WHAT IS PROPHECY?

It is the act of communicating something from the heart or mind of God in the present and leading to a fulfilment in either the immediate or longer-term future – 2 Peter 1:20-21; 1 Tim. 4:14.

What have been your experiences of prophecy? Of hearing it spoken, of giving a prophetic word or of receiving one?

What is your response to Paul's encouragement to, 'eagerly desire the spiritual gifts, especially that you may prophesy?'

_____

_____

_____

_____

_____

Prophetic words have greatly blessed many people's lives, but such words either wrongly given or poorly presented have at times caused difficulty. The answer is never to throw away or even limit a valuable gift that God has given, but take Scriptural instruction to test all prophecy and then to develop in the practice of both receiving and delivering prophecy well.

Types of prophetic expression

There are various types of prophetic expression that come to us in three main categories; as dreams, visions, and words. All will be in accord with the Person and purpose of Jesus Christ (Hebrews 1:1-2).

Dreams: We all dream; it is one way that our sub-conscious mind sorts out the stuff it has been bombarded with and is now processing. We will often dream about the activities and conversations that took place that day, even if the dreams seem quite mixed up and bizarre. Even these dreams can tell us something about how we are feeling, thinking and responding to what is going on around us. However, there other dreams that appear different, more vivid and have a sense of the Lord's activity in them.

I have experienced many such dreams over the years. These have included 'battle dreams' where I seem to be engaged in some warfare situation. These can be quite disturbing but have often alerted me to the schemes of the enemy. There have been dreams that seem to develop God's call on my life often involving cars or other vehicles, where I might have a new car or a larger vehicle, or even have my car stolen. Other dreams have been about people or specific situations, and I sometimes then come across that person or situation the following day. There can be such a variety to this and these dreams often contain key symbolic images.

It is important to pay attention to any such dreams, writing them down as soon as possible, and taking time to seek the Lord over an understanding of their meaning and application. The Bible contains many accounts of God speaking to people in dreams.

Visions: Visions are a bit like dreams except we are awake! Some are clearer than others; some are more detailed than others. It may just be a mental image of something that comes to you as you pray, or a whole scene that the Spirit opens up to you along the lines of Peter's vision of the sheet full of unclean animals (Acts 10:9-16). In the same story the Roman centurion, Cornelius, had a vision in which an angel spoke with him. I woke up one morning, some months before the Covid-19 pandemic began, and 'saw' the word 'REST' in large letters become the word 'RESET.' Over the coming months and the next year, we came into an enforced rest from many activities, and the word reset has been commonly used.

Words: While dreams and visions come in pictorial form they need understanding and expressed in language, in words. Many times, prophecy simply comes as words. We sense the Lord speaking. Often this begins as a sense of something which actually becomes clearer when we begin to verbalise it. I have experienced three main categories of this over the years:

First, on rare occasions I have heard what seemed to be like an audible voice. I am not sure if it was or not, and that is not what is important. The crucial thing was that God spoke, in a short phrase, and the fruit each time was of great transformation. On one such occasion, in the middle of the night, I 'heard' the words, 'you have cursed yourselves as a poor church.' I knew that was for the local church I was pastoring at that time. As I shared this with my three elders, they each in turn recognised how we had done this. Being located in one of the more deprived areas of our city people had often said such things as, 'we'll always struggle' or 'we'll always be poor as a church.' We responded in repentance, agreeing with God's verdict and broke the power of those words of curse. The immediate and longer-term result of financial increase and resourcefulness was remarkable and quite inexplicable from a human viewpoint.

Second, as I have been seeking the Lord over some matter, or waiting before Him, I have sensed what I might call a quickening in my spirit and a thought in the form of unspoken words come to mind. Of course, this could be my own thinking, but at times it has appeared out of the blue and in language that I would not naturally use. As I sat quietly one evening, I suddenly sensed the phrase, 'loose healing a sign of the kingdom' come strongly into my mind. That was not language I would have used at that time and I sensed God was speaking and commissioning. Subsequent events over the next few days confirmed this to me and led to us beginning the Healing Rooms ministry in Scotland. The next ten years brought forth much fruit of healing, salvation and the equipping of many believers.

The third way I have found words coming is when I have prophesied over people. When preaching or teaching I am sometimes drawn to certain people and have a sense of a word for them forming in me. I do not usually know the full extent of this but simply begin speaking out what I have for them and more will follow. My wife, Helen, similarly gets drawn to certain individuals or families, but she will often see something upon them and describes what the Spirit of God is showing her.

There are more ways that God operates than any one of us may know and He will work differently with different people. We must not restrict the moving of the Spirit by any of our pre-conceived notions or our presumption.

We do of course test everything as instructed in 1 Thessalonians 5:19-22. We are to store some things in our heart and wait for God's timing to speak them. We seek understanding and clarification from the Lord. We test according to the bedrock of Scripture and the revelation of the Living Word, Jesus Christ. We submit these words to the church and its leaders to see if there is a witness in the Spirit. We look for the good fruit, though of course some fruit takes a while to grow! The prophetic word encourages and exhorts, and even challenges, but it does not condemn.

The Purpose of Prophecy

Paul states the purpose of prophecy in the church gathering in 1 Corinthians 14:3 as 'edification and exhortation and consolation.' We find in Scripture examples of prophecy that are to warn of danger and enemy activity (Acts 11:27-30; 21:10-11; 2 Kings 6:8-12). It is to encourage and call forth, sometimes activating that which is dormant, unclaimed, or unrealised, releasing faith to receive. Prophecy may often confirm what God has spoken, thereby arousing our heart and giving confidence and courage to step out. When Helen and I heard the Lord calling us to step out from pastoring to begin a new ministry where we would have no salary and had to move from the church manse into rented accommodation, several prophetic words were given to us by people we did not know as a means of confirmation and encouragement.

GROWING IN THE PROPHETIC

We are to seek the Lord and to grow up in Him in all things. And part of that is to grow up in what His word tells us to earnestly desire. Four key aspects in the prophetic process are: **revelation, understanding, language and expression.**

We hear and see in part. We have the Bible (the *logos* or written word of God) but that itself requires some degree of interpretation. There are many varied understandings of certain passages of

Scripture. We have the Holy Spirit who at times brings the *rhema*, that is the spoken word of God today. The Spirit communicates to our spirit but then this is translated to and through our mind, will, and emotions. By the time we speak or deliver a word from God it has worked its way through those aspects of our being and there will be something of us in it. That is one of the reasons why the prophetic word is never placed on a par with the Written Word.

We receive **revelation** in various forms – mainly dreams, visions and words; we then set ourselves to seek the Lord for **understanding** and wisdom about what do with what He shows us, and timing of when to deliver it. We need the Spirit to teach us **language** and we ourselves should seek to develop good language for beneficial communication. Finally, we give **expression** to what we sense the Lord is saying.

How to develop this process?
*Be expectant, God is speaking and all of us can partner with Him. Don't be limited by your past experience but develop an expectation level based on the revelation of God's Word.
*Be observant – listen, watch and wait (Proverbs 8:34), developing an observant spirit that notices things, that picks up on the out of the ordinary as Moses did with the burning bush. Such a bush on fire would not have been uncommon in the hot, dry desert, but Moses noticed that though it burned it was not consumed, and so explored further leading to a dynamic, life-changing encounter with God.
*Seek to remove prejudice and presumption. David is a great example of one who always sought and inquired of the Lord, which was part of his heart's one desire (Psalm 27:4). We find in 2 Samuel 5:17-25 that as he fought the Philistines David enquired of the Lord.

God led him; David defeated them but the same enemy returned later. One might presume to attack them as before but not David. He enquired once more, and the Lord directs him in a very different tactic of war!

*Be in the Word and be impressed with Jesus, beholding Him in His beauty. Growing in the prophetic must be matched by spending significant time in reading, studying and meditating on the Word of God, sitting at His feet to listen and to worship.

How do we deliver prophecy well?

We offer what God gives us; we don't force it upon people. We do not need a preface of 'thus saith the Lord', nor should we seek to adopt an Old Testament model. We always speak and act in love. Be yourself, there is no need to put on some act or 'prophetic performance' and don't try to impress anyone. Give what you get, say what you see – don't add to it or feel the need to pad it out. God can say a lot in a few words!

If you have waited on the Lord, sought and received understanding then present this with confidence coated in humility.

Moving from promise to fulfilment

Clem Ferris, in his book *Stewarding Prophecy*, says, "When we receive a prophecy from the Lord, it is not only a word coming to you, but a word growing in you as you journey through this prophetic process." We are to partner with the word towards its fulfilment. Ferris encourages us to allow the prophetic word to begin a conversation with the Lord where we seek Him with many questions. Too often people want to be told everything right away when the Lord is leading us on a path of delightful discovery.

Prophecy can be like a promise which will produce first fruits then a harvest or fulfilment. We see this again in David's life. God rejects Saul as king and Samuel anoints the young lad David to be the new king of Israel. However, many years pass and Saul is still king. Has Samuel's word failed? Is he a false prophet? Absolutely not! None of Samuel's words 'fell to the ground' but there would be a long prophetic process involved for David. There would be a measure of fruit along the way as he kills the lion and the bear, then slays Goliath. But it is years later before he is crowned king of Judah, then a further delay before being crowned king of all Israel.

In the process we must take hold of what God has said, persevering in belief, becoming fully convinced like Abraham (Romans 4:20-21). We continue to do what the Lord has given us to do now, like David tending his father's flocks, as we await what is to come. We position ourselves to be ready for the initial fruit, as David put himself up there to take on Goliath, trusting that the time for fulfilment is surely coming closer.

Why is prophecy important in the house of prayer?
Paul Billheimer states, 'true prayer starts in the heart of God' and Oswald Chambers said, 'prayer is the point where the reality of God merges with human life.' Prayer is not all about us getting something from God or moving His hand to act on our behalf. In truth, prayer starts with God revealing Himself and His intended will to those who are waiting on Him. Prayer begins with revelation from heaven that grips our hearts causing us to seek Him, to pursue Him for understanding, and where the Spirit gives us the language to express this back to God as a prayer. In this understanding of prayer, the prophetic hearing from God is of great importance. We pray and call forth the Word and will of God on earth. We pray the

prayers of Scripture and we call forth it's promises. Led by the Spirit of God we pray and call forth His will on earth as it is in heaven.

Response:

Think about when God has communicated with you in any of the
ways described in this chapter:

Dreams

_____

_____

_____

_____

_____

Visions

_____

_____

_____

_____

_____

Words

_____

_____

_____

_____

_____

Prophecy given to you

_____

_____

_____

_____

_____

Are you working through the process of these towards their fulfilment?

Take one and write it out again as fully as you can. Ponder and pray over it, asking God lots of questions, discovering its fuller meaning and application, and how you might see its fulfilment.

6. INTERCESSORY PRAYER

We build the house of prayer as we express praise and adoration in response to the grace of the Lord Jesus and the love of the Father with the help and partnership of the Holy Spirit. As we worship and wait, sitting at His feet, gazing on His beauty, He draws us into involvement in releasing His will and kingdom on the earth. God is looking for someone who will agree with Him and speak out here on earth calling forth the unfolding of His eternal purpose in Christ. This is the activity of intercessory prayer.

There are various types of prayer. Ephesians 6:18 says, "with all prayer and petition pray at all times in the Spirit, and with this in view, be alert with all perseverance and petition for all the saints". So, we bring our requests to God for personal needs; we present petitions on behalf of others; we give thanks; we listen; we express love and worship to Him, and more.

Sometimes we are praying to God and other times we are praying with God. On occasion we are asking God for something or to move on our behalf, and there are occasions when in line with His Word and led by His Spirit we are authorising His will on earth. We are joint-heirs with Christ and He has delegated authority to us. He took back the authority that the evil one had usurped in the garden, and He has all authority in heaven and on earth. He now looks for us, who are new creations in Him and filled with His Spirit, to partner with Him to plant the things of heaven on the earth, joining with Him in exercising that authority on the earth, like counter signing the cheque the Father has written and Jesus has signed. As Pete Greig suggests in *Dirty Glory*, 'it is not so much greater activity in prayer that we need but greater authority'.

We are not heard or effective in prayer by our many words, but as we are moved by the Spirit of God, pray in faith, and exercise our God-given authority. We do not ask God to do for us what he has already given us authority to do.

What is Intercessory Prayer?

There is a difference between the term 'intercession' and 'intercessory prayer' – one is a place and the other is a practice. Intercession means to stand between or go between two parties; it is a place that is occupied by someone. Christ is the ultimate intercessor as He eternally occupies the place between God and humanity, standing in the gap between heaven and earth enabling us to engage in intercessory prayer in His name (Hebrews 7:25).

Intercessory prayer is the activity that is based on the position of the Mediator and flows from His mediation. In his book Intercessory Prayer, Dutch Sheets gives this definition: "*Intercessory prayer is an extension of the ministry of Jesus through His Body, the Church, whereby we mediate between God and humanity for the purpose of reconciling the world to Him, or between Satan and humanity for the purpose of enforcing the victory of Calvary.*"

Therefore, our intercessory prayer activity must be relationship based – with Father, Son and Spirit, and with one another. There is a necessity for alignment and agreement with heaven and among the people of God (Matthew 18:19-20). We pray in response to God, becoming proactive on earth, rather than always praying in reaction to what is already happening.

We take our stand as we have been positioned with Jesus, seated with Him in heavenly places (Ephesians 2:6). We are seated, resting in His completed works, His ultimate victory, and also, we stand on earth bringing forth the fruit of His victory in His eternal purpose of redemption. Together with Christ and one another we are fulfilling our priestly role and kingdom expression:

You have made them to be a kingdom and priests to our God; and they will reign upon the earth (Revelation 5:10).

We are representing Him now on earth and reigning with Him in life now and forevermore (Romans 5:17).

Jesus has restored the original mandate of Genesis 1:26-28. We were created in God's likeness, and though greatly marred by sin we are now being formed as new creations into the likeness of His Son. From a heart of devotion to Jesus and worship of Him we carry His authority on the earth to bring the rule of His kingdom: "Your kingdom come, Your will be done, on earth as it is in heaven" (Matthew 6:10). We don't rule over other people, we don't dominate or oppress, but release the life-giving reign of the Lord overcoming all the destructive forces of darkness.

This is a great commission indeed, and one for which we need the partnering power and enabling abilities of the Holy Spirit. Paul says, "the Spirit also helps us in our weakness: for we do not know how to pray as we should, but the Spirit Himself intercedes for us with groanings too deep for words" (Romans 8:26). This prayer starts in the heart of God and is breathed into us by the revelation of the Spirit, who in turn moves with us releasing various expressions of intercessory activity in and through us.

These expressions will include spoken words as the Spirit leads and reveals to us the will of God in various situations. It may come as Paul suggests here in Romans as groans too deep for words. Paul also refers to birthing and travailing (Galatians 4:19) as we carry the seed of God towards its fulfilment. At times we are moved to pray in tongues, even at some length until a sense of breakthrough comes. On occasion we can almost be passive as the Spirit prays through us where we are an instrument of intercession on the earth.

Some of the above expressions imply a battle to bring the breakthrough of the will of God to manifest upon the earth. At times the prayer of faith will yield immediate results, yet at other times there seems to be a delay and a sense of opposition holding up the delivery. This was Daniel's experience as we read in Daniel 10:10-14, where his prayer was heard in heaven immediately and the answer similarly released, but the coming forth of its fulfilment on earth to Daniel was resisted and held up by 'the prince of the kingdom of Persia' who was not a human prince but a ruling demonic spirit over that area.

Likewise, Elijah after his victory on Mount Carmel over Baal worship, got into a birthing position as he called forth the rains. It took sending his servant seven times to look for the answer before the cloud the size of a man's hand appeared (1 Kings 18:41-45). Elijah had heard the sound from heaven which no one else had. In accordance with that revelation, he interceded calling the promised rains to come.

There is no resistance to the will of God in heaven. But there is resistance in the earthly realm, both by demonic spirits in the lower heavenlies (not God's heaven) and by people through unbelief and other sin or opposition. It is these resisting factors that we need to take our stand against and battle through in the power of the Spirit.

How do conduct ourselves in this battle?
This battle, often referred to as spiritual warfare, is spoken of in the New Testament (e.g., Ephesians 6:10-18; 2 Corinthians 10:3-6) and we are given many lessons on battle from the actual wars and conflicts in the Old Testament. Paul says he fought wild beasts in Ephesus (1 Corinthians 15:32) which were clearly not lions and tigers but spirits behind those who opposed him and the gospel.

The Old Testament battles teach us valuable lessons on battling God's way and doing warfare with heaven's wisdom and tactics which often made little sense to the rational mind. Joshua marched the army around Jericho thirteen times before unleashing a shout; Jehoshaphat's army marched out led by priests singing praise; David waited to listen for the sound of an unseen army marching in the treetops; and Moses raised the staff of God on a hilltop enabling Joshua to defeat the Amalekites in the valley.

A first key to warring in spiritual battles is to enquire of and listen to the Lord, and do it His way! He rarely does things the same way twice so we can't write a seven-step formula for success but we battle from a place of relationship with Him.

It is easy to fall into being focussed on what the enemy is doing but we must maintain a God-centred and Christ-focussed attitude in all our battling. We worship the Living God! We remain impressed with Jesus so we will not be intimidated by the enemy. We take our stand on earth because Jesus is seated in the highest place. We declare and do what He tells us, and like Moses we are to 'stand by and see the salvation of the LORD which He will accomplish for you today' (Exodus 14:13). We don't give in to fear but stand in faith.

Once I was in a small town praying along with a small group of believers. As we walked praying around the place, I noticed several signs of occult activity. As we came to a row of shops the local folks pointed out an occult shop which seemed to hold a strong sway over many people. They expressed a sense of fear as they stood on the opposite side of the road. I sensed the Lord instruct me to take them across the road, lay hands on the shop and declare its closure in the name of Jesus Christ. We did, and I heard a week or two later that the shop had now closed and the people running it had moved out of town! The victory of Jesus against darkness had been enforced.

The model of the Tabernacle of David

We began this section with the express desire of David in Psalm 27:4 to behold the beauty of the LORD and to seek and enquire of Him. David was a man after God's heart despite his flaws and failings. He led the nation from a foundation of worshipping the Lord their God.

He brought the Ark of the Covenant up to Jerusalem and provided a simple open tent to house it in. David set up singers and musicians to minister to the Lord both day and night in the sight of all the people. He brought together praise and prophetic declarations (1 Chronicles 25:1-3). Amos the prophet declared that God would restore this tent of David (Amos 9:11-12) and in the New Testament the apostles saw the fulfilling of this as they recognise in Acts 15:16-17:

After these things I will return,
And I will rebuild the tabernacle of David which has fallen,
And I will rebuild its ruins,
And I will restore it,
So that the rest of mankind may seek the Lord,
And all the Gentiles who are called by My name.

This is linked to bringing the Gentiles to salvation, and so we see this restored Tabernacle of David today bringing together praise, prophetic declaration, intercessory prayer and the key to open and shut doors in Jesus' name leading to the great commission.

In the book of Revelation, we see a picture of harps and bowls representing the flow of intermingled songs of worship and prayers (Revelation 5:8). As we sing our praise, and our new songs worshipping the Lamb, we are rightly focussed on Him, energised and strengthened to press in praying and filling these bowls in heaven which will one day be poured out leading to a great move of salvation on the earth.

A PRACTICE OF INTERCESSORY PRAYER

Set aside a time and give yourself to this:

    a) Beholding the beauty of the LORD – Psalm 27:4; 2 Corinthians 3:18.

As we have discussed before, begin focussing on Jesus, worship Him, maybe using certain songs or make up your own! Sense His heart of love towards you and reply with your expressions of adoration and appreciation.

    b) Receiving revelation (wisdom and understanding) – there is an open heaven and open door! Mark 1:10; Matthew 27:51; John 1:51; Revelation 4:1-2

Listen, observe: what are you sensing? A Scripture, or a vision, or a word coming?

Ask questions: What is this? What does it mean? What am I to do in response?

    c) Declaring and announcing His Word – logos and rhema.

Declare God's excellencies (1 Peter 2:9), the truth of Christ's victory and the good news this brings. Declare out loud any word He is giving you.

    d) Calling forth the will of God (battling and birthing) – Galatians 4:19

Now stand on that word from the Lord. Praise Him for the fulfilment that will come on earth even as it is in heaven. Pray with the Holy Spirit contending against any resistance in this realm. Continue until you sense the breakthrough has been made in the spirit realm or you sense the Lord's hand has lifted. Leave it with God and rest in Him.

PART 3: STEWARDING THE KINGDOM

The time is fulfilled, and the kingdom of God is at hand: repent and believe in the gospel
Mark 1:15

Jesus' life and ministry flowed out from His relationship with His Father, the empowering of the Holy Spirit, and His life of prayer. He comes on the public scene proclaiming the good news of God and declaring the immediacy of the kingdom of God.

He calls for a two-fold response:
1. To repent – that is to turn around in your thinking; to change the way that you think; to align with His view of a whole new reality.
2. To believe in the gospel or good news. This good news is variously termed throughout the New Testament as the gospel of God, of Christ, of grace and of the kingdom. Jesus primarily preached the good news of the kingdom of God.

What is the kingdom of God?
It is the realm of God's life-giving rule which was demonstrated by Jesus in His authority over all destructive powers – of demons, disease and finally death. It is good news of the availability of forgiveness for sin through Jesus, and ultimately eternal life.

We see five main aspects of the kingdom:
1. The proximity of the kingdom: It is at hand, or has come near. Elsewhere Jesus says the kingdom is among you and within you. It is now and yet still coming. The time is fulfilled for its commencement on earth, but its fulfilment is still future. Therefore, we can both take hold of it now, and always believe for and expect more to come.
2. There is both an invitation and challenge presented by the kingdom. Jesus invites us into the adventure and discovery

of the kingdom as He issues the invitation to 'come.' He also issues a challenge to 'follow Me'.

3. The kingdom is good news. There is no bad news of the kingdom of God. God is good and His coming kingdom is good news. His kingdom triumphs over the domain of darkness. There is no dualism between light and darkness. The light overcomes; the victory of Christ is certain and secured for all eternity.

4. The kingdom of God is made manifest and visible; it looks like something. It looks like a tormented man being set free, or a sick woman being healed, or even a dead child being raised to life again. It looks like oppression being turned to opportunity, and injustice being redeemed.

5. The kingdom keeps on growing and expanding. Jesus told many parables to show what the kingdom of God is like including images of seed that grows and increases, and of yeast that spreads through the dough.

Stewarding the kingdom:

Jesus said: "*For whoever has, to him more shall be given, and he will have an abundance; but whoever does not have, even what he has shall be taken away from him.*"
Matthew 13:12

Alan Scott in his book *Scattered Servants* says, "Stewardship is the intentional process whereby we learn to increase and expand what God has entrusted to us."

We have been brought into an amazing relationship with God where He keeps us and blesses us in His covenant love. With this privilege comes a responsibility to give away what we receive, knowing there's always more. We have a responsibility to use the gifts and understanding we have been given for the benefit of others. We are to manage God's interests and concerns for the world around us, following after the example of Jesus.

The verse above relates a principle of the kingdom: the one who has and uses it will be given more responsibility and more to use (see also Matthew 25:14-30). The one who doesn't use what he has been entrusted with in a sense does not have anything because he has failed to take hold of it for its proper purpose. So even what he has which he doesn't use will be taken from him. The message is plain: take hold of and steward well what God has entrusted to you and you will be given an abundance!

As we follow Jesus' example and ministry there were three primary kingdom activities that He engaged in, and which He equipped and sent His disciples out to do them as well:
1. Announcing (preaching, proclaiming) the good news
2. Taking authority over evil spirits and freeing people from them
3. Healing the sick

Jesus' ministry was all about doing the will of His Father which is bringing good news to the people. After trying to get time alone with His disciples, Jesus is surrounded once again by the crowds. Even though it is inconvenient and unplanned He still welcomes them, speaks to them about the kingdom of God and cures those in need of healing (Luke 9:10-11).

To welcome and value people is a necessary starting point, one we can all be involved in and can get better at doing. In this section we will learn about announcing the kingdom's good news, taking and exercising the authority Jesus has given us over all demons, and healing sickness of body, soul and spirit.

7. ANNOUNCING THE GOOD NEWS

Our world is filled with bad news narratives. It appears that the media feeds on this, relating the most dramatic, and at times depressing stories. These are fear producing and anxiety inducing which insidiously grips people's minds and emotions. We also hear bad news at a personal level as we hear of friends and others we know diagnosed with cancer or other serious illness. Our reactions can be of despair or of seeking to block these out or we can even become increasingly immune to their effect.

While not denying the vast amount of human suffering we need to understand and announce the Biblical message that there is good news! In truth, there is always more good news than bad news. There is more grace than sin. Jesus' ultimate victory stands forever and 'His blood speaks a better word' (Hebrews 12:24). There may be more people telling bad news, like the ten spies who gave a bad report, but the good report of the two spies outweighed them. Likewise, our announcing of good news will outweigh the vast sea of dread-filled reports.

So, what is the good news?
What does it mean to announce it?
How and when and where do we do this?
What are we up against?
And what does this announcement to lead to?

Let's start with Jesus and His twelve disciples.

And He appointed twelve, so that they would be with Him and that He could send them out to preach. Mark 3:14

It always starts with relationship. They were to be with Him and spend time in His presence; listening, watching, being impressed with Him and being His friends and companions. These men He had summoned and called out from among others who would have been around Him. He appoints them, that is He makes them something, designates them, and fashions and prepares them for a special service and purpose. That purpose is to make an announcement like a herald. Similarly, we have been summoned and appointed by Jesus, and now anointed with His Spirit, and we too have been given a message to announce. It's not our message in the sense that we invented it. It is God's message. However, it is also now our message in that we have received it, embraced it and have our own testimony of its outworking in our lives.

What is the good news?

In Biblical times the herald was a messenger who brought the news of a victory, or of political or personal news that caused joy. God's herald announced His universal victory over the world and His kingly rule:

How lovely on the mountains
Are the feet of him who brings good news,
Who announces peace (well-being)
And brings good news of happiness,
Who announces salvation,
And says to Zion, "Your God reigns."
Isaiah 52:7

Jesus takes on the mantle of Isaiah 61:1 of bringing and announcing good news to the afflicted, poor, and oppressed. There is good news for all who have in any way been oppressed by another rule, and that's all of us. It is the good news that God reigns and Jesus displays this powerfully.

In the New Testament this good news or gospel is described in various ways: the gospel of the kingdom (Matthew 4:23; 9:35); the gospel of Jesus Christ (Mark 1:1; Romans 15:19); the gospel of God (Mark 1:14; Romans 1:1); the gospel of God's grace (Acts 20:24); the gospel of your salvation (Ephesians 1:13), the gospel of peace (Ephesians 6:15), and simply the gospel (Mark 1:15; Acts 8:25). They are all essentially different aspects of the same thing.

Jesus sent His disciples to proclaim this good news, and He also sent them and sends us as His witnesses (Acts 1:8). The early disciples viewed themselves as 'witnesses of His resurrection' (Acts 1:22; 4:33), which is the ultimate and conclusive victory that leads to the announcing of good news.

The good news could be described as the victory of God through Christ's death and resurrection over sin, over Satan and over death, and His subsequent reign (kingdom rule) over the oppressive and destructive powers of each of these. It is the good news of forgiveness through Jesus' sacrifice, of newness of life and eternal life through Him.

What are the obstacles to the good news?

The good news is just that - 'good news!' It's wonderful news but it's not always welcomed. In truth, it's not always heard and certainly not always understood. So, what's the problem?

As Paul says to the Corinthians:

Our gospel is veiled, it is veiled to those who are perishing, in whose case the god of this world has blinded the minds of the unbelieving
2 Corinthians 4:3-4

There is a veil that hangs over the minds and hearts of many people. It is a veil that has been caused by the blinding influences of the evil one. There is a battle for the souls of humanity. The good news itself also offends or is a stumbling block to people. It offends the pride of the human heart. Even people who have greatly struggled in life can have a pride in themselves that they can work their way out of the mess.

Two areas that we need to acknowledge and tackle, especially in the western world, is that generally people are not listening to the message of the church, and even when people do hear something they often don't understand it because of their pre-conceived ideas about what it means. In the parable of the Sower who sows the seed of the word (Matthew 13:1-23) Jesus says that some is stolen away immediately, other seed is stifled or choked and does not develop, but some lands in good soil and produces a harvest. The key to this is the one 'who hears the word and understands it' (v23).

How can we overcome these obstacles?
How do we get people to hear and to understand the good news?
First, we need to get people's attention. There may be numerous ways to do this, but it appears the most common way in the New Testament was through signs, wonders and miracles. We read of Philip going to Samaria proclaiming Christ to them:

The crowds with one accord were giving attention to what was said by Philip, as they heard and saw the signs which he was performing Acts 8:6

These signs included the casting out of unclean spirits – people heard the evidence of this; and the healing of many who had been paralysed or lame – the people saw the results of this too. Similarly, throughout the book of Acts we see this pattern again and again. In chapter two, it was the evidence of speaking in other tongues that caused a stir and a crowd to gather and listen; in chapter three, it was the healing of a man who had been lame from birth that drew an attentive crowd once again; in chapter five, it was healings and miracles that caused people to bring the sick and afflicted to where Peter and the apostles were; in chapter nine, it was healing miracles and the raising of the dead that led to villages and towns turning to the Lord; and in chapter fourteen it was the raising of a lame man which gave Paul the opening and opportunity to proclaim the good news of Jesus.

Indeed, Paul later reflects:

My message and my preaching were not in persuasive words of wisdom, but in demonstration of the Spirit and of power
1 Corinthians 2:4

These signs point the way to Jesus. The wonders make people wonder. Throughout Jesus' ministry people were often said to be amazed and astonished when they witnessed the miracles. One of those words originally had the sense of being thrown or shifted out of position. One example is found in Luke 5:26 where the people are 'astonished,' that is the Greek term *ekstasis* which means to throw the mind from its normal state, to break the pattern of a wrong mindset and open up to the truth of the reign of God. This resulted here in the people both glorifying God and being filled with fear.

Such miracles, signs and wonders get attention and bring reaction. It is not always positive, like at Pentecost (Acts 2:13); people don't always come to believe in Jesus, but it cannot be ignored. We don't seek after signs and wonders for any sensation for ourselves but we must seek after them to open up doors of opportunity for the announcing of the good news. This is what the early believers understood and prayed for when the religious authorities had sought to silence them:

And now, Lord, take note of their threats, and grant that Your bond-servants may speak Your word with all confidence, while You extend Your hand to heal, and signs and wonders take place through the name of Your holy servant Jesus Acts 4:29-30.

The prayer was answered spectacularly as the very building shook and they went out and spoke the word with boldness.

Signs and wonders get people's attention but they also give us confidence to speak. The word translated as confidence and then boldness in Acts 4:29 and then 4:31 is the same Greek word. It is a most important term in the book of Acts and has a range of meaning including to speak with ease and freedom; without hindrance or restriction; with confidence and boldness; openly; and to speak everything on one's mind without holding back. It is to freely and fully announce the good news. When God has just healed someone, who is not yet a believer, we usually have their attention and we are emboldened to speak the word of the Lord to them, pointing them to the One who can save completely.

Second, we have to help people to an understanding of the good news that we are announcing to them. This may require the dismantling of some old ideas about 'religion,' or the thoughts conceived through previous unhelpful experience of 'church.' We need to know the grace of God in truth (Colossians 1:6), and how to explain it clearly. The personal understanding and experience of the grace of the Lord Jesus that we explored at the beginning is now to be explained to others. This is not accomplished immediately but unfolded over time, but we must stand on a sure footing of grace that undoes the faulty concepts about God and the Christ-following life.

How and when and where are we to announce it?

Everywhere and somewhere! Jesus sends His witness to the ends of the earth, to all people. Yet, He sent them through Jerusalem, Judea and Samaria first. At one time He sent them only to the lost sheep of Israel (Matthew 10:6), and later He sent them to all nations (Matthew 28:19). Paul had his sphere of ministry (2 Corinthians 10:13-16), and was even prevented by the Spirit of Jesus from entering certain places at a particular time (Acts 16:6-7).

Though we are called and sent to all people we have to start somewhere or we may never start. We are placed in specific situations and can be called to particular groups. There are people who are ready to receive the word and there are those who are very resistant. There are those in whom we plant a small seed, and others might plant more until finally the fruit is ripe.

We are in the time of God's favour and the day of His salvation (2 Corinthians 6:2). Every day is a day of opportunity and possibility in the kingdom of God. It is now time to announce good news, yet we also listen for the prompting of the Spirit to speak the right word at the right time to the right person. To bombard a resistant person may have the effect of getting their back up and increasing their resistance. We are given power to be His witnesses, and the Spirit will not only release signs and wonders but also opens up divine appointments, gives words of wisdom and knowledge about people for us at times to share with them. Expect and look for His openings.

We make the announcement of this good news simply, naturally, and in everyday language, presenting it with relevance and meaningfully. Tell your own story – people like stories as they are not confrontational but invite exploration. Introduce Jesus into the story. Let it sink in. Don't rush to get a response or manufacture anything, but at the right moment ask the pertinent questions.

What does this announcement lead to?

It implants the Word, the testimony of Jesus. It may need some watering and time. The Spirit is at work and grace and truth begin to unfold. It doesn't only ask questions but invites questions: What does this mean? (Acts 2:12) What shall we do? (Acts 2:38). Give people time and space to form and ask their own questions.

The answer is broadly speaking that God is calling this person to Himself. Their response is to repent, believe in the Lord Jesus, be baptised and receive the Holy Spirit (Acts 2:38; 16:31). We explain this in understandable and meaningful language that enables a full response.

What is the purpose of the good news?

The purpose is to announce God's ultimate victory and eternal purpose in Christ Jesus. To show and tell that His kingdom has come and all that has oppressed humankind need no longer hold its destructive influence over us. It is to invite all people into a covenant relationship with God and to be part of a new community of faith in Jesus.

So, we are to follow and fulfil Jesus' command to **make disciples who in turn will make disciples.** The good news effect doesn't finish with a conversion to believing in Jesus. We continually need to hear the full good news into every unbelieving area of our hearts, and we are to announce and teach the fullness of this good news of grace, the love of the Father, and new life in the Spirit to all who do believe that they might grow up into all the fullness of God.

Response

What is your story? How would you tell it and how would you introduce Jesus as the main character? Try writing it out.

Make the prayer of Acts 4:29-30 your own prayer.

What difference would it make to have that God-given confidence and boldness?

What difference would it make if your witness was accompanied by healings, signs and wonders?

Where, when and to whom might you announce this good news?

8. KINGDOM AUTHORITY

One day I was, along with a female member of my prayer team, praying with a woman in my church around some of the struggles she was experiencing. As we touched on a certain area, her appearance suddenly changed and became quite distorted. As she made a few strange sounds, I realised we were dealing with a demon or unclean spirit. Under the influence of the grace and truth of Jesus, and the anointing of the Holy Spirit, and with the two us taking hold of our authority in the name of Jesus, the demon was cast out.

A few moments later she became aware of the need to confess a specific sin, and as she did there was another manifestation of an unclean spirit. It too was evicted in Jesus' name, and the woman involved found a level of freedom she had never before experienced.
We had been introduced to a realm of ministry that we had never known, though it is there throughout the Bible. We witnessed first-hand the victorious name of Jesus over demons, and shared in the wonderful joy that comes when someone is set free.

We return to Jesus' appointment of His disciples in Mark 3:14-15:
He appointed twelve, so that they would be with Him and that He could send them out to preach, and to have authority to cast out the demons.

We emphasise once more that all kingdom works flow out of a deepening relationship with Jesus who then sends us out to announce good news, to cast out demons and to heal the sick. The ministry of healing, while neglected by large sections of the church for centuries, is making a comeback and being widely acknowledged as necessary and right for today. The act of casting out of demons is not so widespread for various reasons, yet was prominent in Jesus' ministry and His sending of His disciples, and is at times a necessary precursor to lasting healing. These three great activities of Jesus' ministry very much go together, working hand in hand, with each one in turn often leading to one of the others. As we announce good news in the power of the Spirit demons tremble and flee, and sicknesses are healed. As the sick are healed, we declare the good news of Jesus as Lord and Saviour, and the oppressed are set free.

Jesus' ministry
That evening they brought to Him many who were oppressed by demons, and He cast out the spirits with a word and healed all who were sick Matthew 8:16 (ESV)
In Mark 1:21-28 we find Jesus teaching in the synagogue. His teaching comes with such authority that an unclean spirit in a man there cannot keep still and cries out in a loud voice. Jesus silencing this spirit casts it out of the man. The people are amazed at His teaching and this display of authority.

On another occasion in a synagogue, while He is speaking to the people, Jesus sees a woman who is all bent over due to a spirit of infirmity. He calls her forward and announces the good news with authority, "Woman, you are freed (loosed) from your sickness (infirmity)" He then lays His hands on her and she immediately straightens up and glorifies God (see Luke 13:10-13).

In Acts 10:38 Peter states in his preaching to Cornelius' household that:
He went about doing good and healing all who were oppressed by the devil, for God was with Him.

The gospels record twenty-two accounts of Jesus healing specific individuals (though He healed many, many more), and in eight of those accounts He does so by means of casting out a spirit.

What can we conclude from this?
Jesus clearly believed that demons (unclean or evil spirits) existed and operated destructively in human lives.

These demons were sometimes, but not always, a cause of certain physical infirmities.
Jesus evicted them promptly by exercising His authority on earth.
This was a significant part of His ministry and one He did not hide away.

The disciples' ministry
We have already noted Jesus' call and the initial commission of His twelve in Mark 3:13-15. Then in Mark 6:7-13 we see them being sent out themselves on a mission trip. As He sent them it says that He, "gave them authority over the unclean spirits" (v7). Verses 12-13 conclude:

They went out and preached that men should repent. And they were casting out many demons and were anointing with oil many sick people and healing them.

Luke 9:1-6 emphasis that:

He ...gave them power and authority over all demons and to heal diseases. And He sent them out to proclaim the kingdom of God and to perform healing (vs1-2).

When we come into Acts, we see great evidence of the power of God through those disciples and others. Such was the evidence of this that the people brought those who were sick and afflicted with unclean spirits to the apostles and they were all healed (Acts 5:16). As already referred to, Philip evicted many demons in Samaria, which along with healing miracles caused a great shift for the gospel in that city (Acts 8:4-8).

What can we conclude from this?
The disciples continued in the authority of Jesus and in the pattern that He had set of casting out spirits and healing.
They were given authority over all demons.
While this is important, their primary focus was on proclaiming the good news and healing people everywhere.

Our ministry
As we continue following Jesus, doing and teaching all that He commanded, so we must announce good news, accompanied by evidences of the power of God in healing and miracles, which will at times require the removal of demonic spirits.

The importance of understanding authority
In the beginning God created the earth, making humankind in His likeness. He gave them permission and a commission to rule over and subdue the other created things on the earth. God delegated this authority to us. But Adam fell and lost this right to rule in God's name. Satan quickly usurped this authority and has wielded it to tragic ends ever since. That was until Jesus came, the Son of God as

a Man, to redeem what the original man, Adam, had lost. Jesus now has all authority in heaven and on earth (Matthew 28:18) and has delegated this authority on earth back to us, His blood redeemed church. As He gave His disciples authority over unclean spirits and to heal sickness, so He has given this to us today. We don't ask the Father to cast out a spirit, we do it! We don't ask God to heal a sick person, Jesus never did, but we heal them in His name. We may lift them up to the Lord in prayer, but we don't ask God to do what He has authorised us to do.

Jesus has won the ultimate victory and Satan is defeated. But the battle still rages with the devil, like with a mortally wounded adversary who seeks to cause as much havoc as he can with the little time he has left. We need to rise up and take hold of the authority given to us. The enemy truly fears a church that not only knows who it is and what it has in Christ, but actually acts on it and exercises the power and authority granted from heaven.

Keys for exercising authority in Jesus' name:
1. Living under Christ's authority so we may exercise His delegated authority (Matthew 8:9). The centurion understood the principle of how authority works. Like him, we only have this authority because of whose authority we are under. We must continually live our lives submitted and aligned to Christ, His Word and His ways.

2. Teach with authority (Matthew 7:29). It was recognised by the people that Jesus taught differently from the scribes of the day, because He taught with an authority that brought reaction on several levels. We too, must teach the Word of God with the anointing of the Spirit that our words too will carry heavenly authority on earth. As we teach with insight and revelation, we uncover the works of demonic spirits, exposing their roots, and enabling great release.

3. Pronounce forgiveness (on account of Jesus) with authority (Matthew 9:6; John 20:23). Jesus had authority on earth to forgive sins and has all authority to do so forever. It can seem too much to suggest we can exercise this authority as indeed only God can forgive sins that are ultimately against Him. However, we know the good news of grace, and when people confess their sins, He is faithful and just to forgive (1 John 1:9). We can announce this to them and pronounce them forgiven on account of Christ. This is often most helpful and releasing for those struggling under a weight of false guilt and shame. It can also release a deceptive grip of the evil one leading to deliverance and freedom.

4. Bind and loose His will on earth (Matthew 16:19; 18:18). We will return to this point again in the final section as we look at the nature of the church, but here we recognise that Jesus associates the keys of the kingdom with binding and loosing, suggesting these are areas which we use authority over. We bind what has been bound in heaven, primarily the work of the evil one, and we loose what has been loosed in heaven, primarily the works of God's kingdom. The context in Matthew 18:15-18 suggests this binding and loosing is more associated with permitting and forbidding, dealing with sin in the church.

5. To cast out demons/unclean spirits and heal the sick (Matthew 10:1). All the above keys prepare us in some way for this kingdom ministry of setting people free from demonic influence, and releasing healing. The verse referred to here says:
Jesus...gave them authority over unclean spirits, to cast them out
There is no point in having authority if we don't use it.

RELEASING FROM DEMONIC INTERFERENCE

He appeared in order to take away our sins
1 John 3:5
The reason the Son of God appeared was to undo (loose) the devil's work
1 John 3:8
He has delivered us from the domain of darkness and transferred us to the kingdom of His beloved Son, in whom we have redemption, the forgiveness of sins
Colossians 1:13-14

Jesus is Victor! He has delivered us; we have been transferred. But we can still remain under the influence of the evil one in some ways where we have not truly believed and appropriated the full good news of grace in Christ.

Jesus undoes the works of the devil, because He is the one who forgives and takes away our sins. Sin gives the evil one a foothold in our lives. If we still believe the lies of condemnation then we can remain bound to them. Grace brings forgiveness and truth defeats lies, and Jesus comes full of grace and truth.

Deliverance – what are we actually talking about?
What are demons?
They are spirit beings, usually referred to as evil or unclean, that operate under Satan's domain and hierarchy. They usually operate in a particular area, for example, infirmity or anger or lust, and so have those names.

How do they affect people?
They are always destructive in some way and seek to harm human life and relationships. They can cause pain and other physical

problems; mental confusion; suicidal thoughts; emotional disturbance and more. However, you can experience any of these by other causes and not demons.

Demons gain an entry point at some time and thereby hold some ground in a person's life. They are intruders who exert an influence. People can be oppressed by a spirit, sometimes to a low degree, and sometimes higher. We do not use the terms 'possession' or 'demon-possessed' though many of our Bible translations unfortunately and inaccurately do this. The Greek term means to be affected by a demon and does not imply full possession. We follow the English Standard Version here which has thankfully avoided the 'possessed' word.

What are the signs of demonic presence?
There are several signs though some of these could be confused with signs of mental or emotional disturbance and care is needed here. Clearer signs of demonic activity are a strong aversion to the name of Jesus, a sudden change in facial appearance when being prayed with, sometimes accompanied by use of unexpected foul language.

Are there different categories of demons?
There appears to be a hierarchy within the demonic ranks under Satan. The Bible speaks of various evil rulers, powers and forces in the spiritual realm (Ephesians 6:12). Our exercising of authority is primarily focussed on the rank-and-file spirits that directly afflict humanity.

Simple and complex deliverance
We use these terms to describe our experience of dealing with demonic spirits in afflicted people. There are simple cases, where a demon causes, for example, infirmity. It may have gained a hold on the person through the trauma of an accident. We cover the single

incident in prayer and evict the spirit. It is not connected to or embroiled in other areas and wounds of the person's soul.

There are more complex situations where there can be a group of spirits operating against a person that may need removed one at a time. There may be what appears as a large knot where demonic influence is tied in with some major inner wounds. It is important to take time to prayerfully untie the knots and bring healing to the wounded areas so that effective deliverance can take place.

On occasions we have been asked to bring cleansing prayer for places particularly where there are unexplained disturbances. This is usually quite straightforward, but always important that any open door or hold the enemy has is first dealt with properly. This may involve historical acts, for example, of violence in a place, or the removal of occult objects from a room. Once cleansed we would pray to dedicate that place for God's purposes.

As we come to a practical outline of how to effectively bring freedom to people by casting out demons it is good to recognise the tools we have in the Lord.

What do you have for the job?
Authority in Christ (Luke 9:1; 2 Corinthians 5:20).
The power of His name (Acts 16:18).
The gifts of the Holy Spirit – especially distinguishing of spirits. Be led by the Holy Spirit, always.
The Word of God – especially related to the blood of Jesus, His victory, and the enemy's defeat.
Praise and prayer. Praying in tongues can be very helpful.
The power of agreement (always minister in twos or teams).
Awareness of the enemy's schemes (2 Corinthians 2:11) – lies, fear, intimidation and threat.

The Three Stages of Deliverance:
A. Preparing the ground:
1. Forgiveness issues (1 John 3:5). Ensure they have confessed sin, received forgiveness and forgive those who have wronged them.
2. Wrong agreements, lies and ungodly beliefs. These need to be recognised, confronted, and repented of and renounced. We replace them with the truth as it is in Jesus.
3. Wounds of the soul, including trauma and shock often related to abuse and accidents. We lift off the effect of trauma in Jesus' name, and minister healing prayer into the exposed wounded areas that the enemy has trafficked in (more on this healing in the next chapter).
4. Close off the entry point – deal with the above areas plus any generational entry points, ungodly soul-ties (that is close or covenant type relationships that have been abusive, controlling etc). Encourage a renouncement of any occult involvement and the removing of any related objects, jewellery etc.

B. Evicting demonic intruders:
When a person comes to Christ demonic 'inhabitants' have their status changed to 'trespassers,' but they still need put out!
1. Have the person participate and co-operate as best they can. Have them pray a prayer of submission to Christ Jesus as Lord.
2. Invite the fresh anointing of the Holy Spirit.
3. Deal with one area at a time.
4. Identify and command the demon to leave (don't shout). Demons leave often through a yawn, a deep sigh, cough or sometimes a scream or shout. Other times they may leave quite silently.

5. Keep the whole session in order; don't let manifestations take over. Treat the person well having regard for their dignity.
6. Check that there is freedom from the afflicting spirit (looking into their eyes as you pray is useful for sensing any indication of something still present).
7. Pray for a filling of the Holy Spirit, especially that they would be filled with His opposite goodness from the activity of the evicted spirit. Pray for the baptism in the Holy Spirit if they haven't already received this.
8. Praise God together and commit all involved to His care and cover.

C. Aftercare:
1. Make sure the person has contact with a Christian community.
2. Encourage them to draw near to God and guard their heart.
3. Ensure they know to resist any fresh assaults of the enemy, encouraging them to use the power of praise, the word of God and their testimony.
4. Arrange a follow up session where appropriate.

Seeing people set free, sometimes from years of bondage, is a glorious ministry that brings much joy. It is not to be entered into lightly or carelessly, but with good preparation in the Lord. When we are truly under His authority, we can exercise authority. Filled with and led by the Holy Spirit, working together as teams under godly leadership, and following wise procedures we can grow in experience and be effective in setting the captives free.

Response

What shifts need to happen in your understanding and in your life life for you to function more fully in the authority that Christ has delegated to His people?

_____

_____

_____

_____

What will you do about this?

_____

_____

_____

_____

9. HEALING

Mary came into the building where we ran a Healing Room on a dark, dreary, dismal evening. The outside conditions were a bit like how she felt. Her body was riddled with arthritic pain, she was quite despondent, and in her words, she had 'lost her faith.' But the kingdom of God was at hand, and Mary was about to encounter Jesus afresh and the power of His Spirit.

We welcomed Mary and put her at ease. She had been brought along by a friend and didn't have any real expectation for what could happen. We listened to her story and then invited her to stand. We blessed her and welcomed the anointing of the Holy Spirit. He doesn't disappoint and waves of His peace and love came over this dear woman. The despondency left and was replaced by lovely sense of joy as Mary broke forth in laughter. Sensing the pleasure and goodness of God, she promptly turned to Him afresh and found the faith of Jesus anew. She was feeling wonderful and ready to go on her way. I suggested that having come in suffering crippling pain she should not leave still carrying it within her. We laid hands over her and within seconds the hovering Spirit of God moved gently yet powerfully through her body. Pain vanished in His presence. Her right hand was badly crippled and bound in a support. She told us that she had not been able to hold a pen or pencil to write in over two years! We watched as the snarled-up joints loosened and the hand became totally free.

Mary returned to our reception area where she took hold of a pen and wrote a full-page account of what the Lord had just done for her. Then she stood and raised her arms up above her head. At that moment, her friend came out from the room where she had been receiving prayer and observed Mary with her hands held high. The friends' mouth dropped open, then she exclaimed, "You can't do that!" She was wonderfully shocked by the transformation in her friend.

Healing, or to be made well, is part of the fruit of salvation. The New Testament word for salvation, *sozo*, is at times used to speak of physical healing and well-being (e.g., Mark 5:28). It is similar in meaning to the Old Testament Hebrew word, *shalom*. This term is often translated as peace, but is much further reaching than our general sense of peace. It means wholeness, well-being and security.

Jesus heals the whole person. That dark night Mary received physical, emotional and spiritual healing. Jesus is concerned for and sufficient for our whole being. There is healing in the name of Jesus, in His Person and through His works. There is healing through covenant relationship; in and through the kingdom of God coming, and through the power and presence of the Holy Spirit. There is much healing through the reconciling effect of the grace of Jesus Christ, and through receiving the unending love of the Father.

There are a variety of forms of healing and a diversity of ways in which it comes. Interestingly, when Paul speaks of the different gifts of the Spirit, they are all expressed as for example, the gift of prophecy, knowledge, faith etc. Except healing, where he says, 'gifts of healings' (1 Corinthians 12:9).

*Healing is a sign of the kingdom and as we mentioned before acts as a sign and wonder capturing people's attention and drawing them to the Lord.

*There are immediate miracles of healing where someone is instantly healed. We have seen this where, for example, a diagnosed tumour 'disappears' straight after a moment of healing prayer, and is confirmed by a scan or tests.

*There is a healing process which of course we see naturally many times as our God-designed bodies recover from ailments, illnesses, or accidents. That healing process can at times be blocked and healing prayer brings the necessary release for it to happen.

*There is healing of the body, healing of the emotions and painful memories, healing of the mind and healing of the spirit. These are often inter-related.

Healing in the ministry of Jesus

Jesus was going throughout all Galilee, teaching in their synagogues and proclaiming the gospel of the kingdom, and healing every kind of disease and every kind of sickness among the people. Matthew 4:23

He...healed all who were ill. This was to fulfil what was spoken through Isaiah the prophet: "HE HIMSELF TOOK OUR INFIRMITIES AND CARRIED AWAY OUR DISEASES" Matthew 8:16-17

And large crowds came to Him, bringing with them those who were lame, crippled, blind, mute, and many others, and they laid them down at His feet: and He healed them. Matthew 15:30

These are just a small selection of the great number of gospel verses that speak about and give account of Jesus healing people from all manner of sickness and disease. It was unarguably a significant part of what Jesus did.

He was fulfilling Old Testament prophecy, such as Isaiah 35:5-6 and 53:4-5. Those latter verses often contain the translations 'griefs' and 'sorrows,' but the Hebrew words can equally be translated as 'sickness' and 'pains.' Jesus heals them all!

He was revealing the nature of His Father, Israel's covenant God, who had named Himself the LORD who heals (Exodus 15:26) or 'I, the LORD, am your healer.' Jesus brings the full revelation of God in every way.

He was bringing the kingdom of God on earth as a foretaste of how it will be in heaven, when, "there will no longer be any death; there will no longer be any mourning, or crying, or pain" (Revelation 21:4). He was revealing Himself as the King of this kingdom.

We may accept the accounts of Jesus' healings and miracles as true, but believe they were for that time and not for today. However, there is absolutely no Scriptural evidence that these things have been done away with, and we see many evidences today of their continuation to the glory of Christ. We may believe Jesus healed in such a manner because He was God in the flesh, and He was indeed. Yet, He came as a man, fully man, sinless and righteous, and filled with the Holy Spirit. He healed through the anointing and power of the Spirit. He created the same opportunity for His disciples, and for us! We are cleansed of our sin and made righteous before God, and we are baptised in the Holy Spirit. The key is believing this and receiving the fullness of this. We were not sinless, but we are forgiven. We still have the memory of our faulty ways and thinking, so we have to keep reckoning ourselves dead to sin and alive to God (Romans 6:11). We have to grow up in the faith of Christ. We are learning and we learn best as we do what he has commanded us to do. We don't minister healing for any other reason than that Jesus sends and commands us to do this.

Healing in the ministry of His disciples and the early church

Jesus sent His followers to do what He did. Not only the twelve, but at least seventy others on another occasion (see Luke 9:1-6 and 10:1-9). He sends all of us who believe in Him, and that is the qualifying factor:

These signs will accompany those who have believed; in My name...they will lay hands on the sick and they will recover. Mark 16:17-18

This continues at a new pace in the book of Acts:

Also, the people from the cities in the vicinity of Jerusalem were coming together, bringing people who were sick or afflicted with unclean spirits, and they were all being healed. Acts 5:16

Many and various healings took place at the hands of the apostles and others in those days (Acts 3:1-10; 8:4-8; 9:32-40; 14:8-10; 20:9-12; 28:7-9). These were often key in breaking new ground for announcing the good news of Jesus.

Four Keys in Healing

We discover four keys in Jesus' healing works that were passed on to His disciples and are most important for us.

Authority

We have spoken about this key foundation for healing in the last chapter. Jesus has authority over everything which includes every sickness, disease or infirmity. He delegates His authority to us to act as His representatives to release His healing on earth. We can pray for sick people, lifting them up to God, and laying them at the feet of Jesus. But we also must recognise that we are authorised to heal the sick. So, we don't keep asking God to do what he expects and has permitted us to do.

Power

Coupled with this authority is the power of God. He empowers those He authorises. Luke 5:17 says, "the power of the Lord was present for Him to perform healing," and Luke 6:19 relates that, "power was coming from Him and healing them all." We receive power when the Holy Spirit comes upon us, and we release His power into our broken world. We are conduits of His power to heal.

Faith

Jesus emphasised the importance of faith, and encouraged its development. When two blind men approached Him, Jesus asked them if they believed He was able to restore their sight, and at their affirmative reply, the Lord declares, "it shall be done to you according to your faith" (Matthew 9:29). Jesus encourages Jairus to 'only believe' or 'keep on believing' as it may also be translated in Mark 5:36. After the healing of the lame man, Peter states that this came about "on the basis of faith in His name" (Acts 3:16). James writes that the "prayer of faith will restore the one who is sick" (James 5:15). This isn't a faith that we work up or try hard to achieve, but it is the faith of the Son of God that we have received and now release its effect.

Compassion

Jesus fully reflected the character of God (Hebrews 1:3), and one of those characteristics that is very much related to healing is compassion (Exodus 34:6; Luke 15:20). As Jesus encounters a leper, we read in Mark 1:41:

Then Jesus, moved with compassion, stretched out His hand and touched him, and said to him, "I am willing; be cleansed."

Jesus was moved with or filled with compassion. The Greek word is *spagchnizomai* —sounds gut wrenching - and it is! It means to be moved in one's inward parts; to be indignant (anger at disease and its affects) and to be moved to action, to bring change and healing. It is very different from sympathy which comes into agreement with sickness and hinders healing.

Questions that Jesus Asked

1. **'Do you want to get well?' (John 5:6).** This is a really important question! Sometimes people want a 'touch' from God but don't actually want healed. Some have issues with the loss of what they see as various benefits of their condition. This question cuts through any self-pity that a person may be trapped in.

2. **'What do you want me to do for you?' (Mark 10:51).** Jesus asks this of a blind man – the answer seemed obvious, but Jesus draws out from the man what he really wants, and at the same time gives the man the dignity to say what he wants rather than just presuming. It is very helpful to begin by asking the person to very specifically state what they want the Lord to do for them.

3. **'Do you believe I am able to do this?' (Matthew 9:28).** Again, a crucial question as faith is so important in healing. If a person has faith (even if it is as a mustard seed) then it is good for them to declare this and let it grow. If they lack faith then we must encourage them in faith through the word of Christ (Romans 10:17) and through testimony.

4. **'How long has he been like this?' (Mark 9:21).** In this episode where first the disciples had failed to free and heal the boy; Jesus engages in conversation with the boy's father. He asks a question to gain understanding of the condition. We will often ask questions to try to better understand the source and root of a condition,

and in turn how we are to proceed in ministry. We ask questions alongside listening for insight from the Spirit.

5. **'Do you see anything?' (Mark 8:23).** In this instance the man is partially healed at the first touch of Jesus but has not fully received his sight. Jesus asks a question to discover what is happening and what difference there might be. We should always ask people what is happening, how they feel now, is there any pain or whatever is appropriate. If they are not fully healed continue until full healing comes.

Jesus' questions cut to the chase and expose some of the blockages to healing and the root causes of conditions. It is so important that we understand that these blockages exist and how to remove them or else we will often find ourselves disappointed at a lack of healing. We are to receive His authority and power, cultivate faith in ourselves and others, be filled with compassion, and grow in wisdom and understanding from the Lord.

BLOCKAGES TO HEALING

Unbelief

Jesus encouraged people to have faith in God, to believe and keep on believing. We can have faith and on occasion still doubt. Jesus encouraged faith AS a mustard seed (Matthew 17:20). The text does not say faith the size of a mustard as if tiny sized faith was good, but faith as a mustard seed, that may start small but has the properties of the mustard seed to grow into something much more. We don't ever scold people for their lack of faith but encourage the development and expression of faith.

Unbelief is altogether different. It is a fixed position or spirit of the mind that won't believe in what God can do in a given situation. Jesus clearly saw this as a hindrance to the flow of His power, and we find Him in Mark 5:37-43 putting out the unbelieving people before raising the daughter of Jairus from the dead.

A key passage about the blocking power of unbelief is in **Mark 6:1-6** where Jesus could do no miracles in his home town because of the people's unbelief:
And He could do no miracle there except that He laid hands on a few sick people and healed them. And He wondered at their unbelief Mark 6:5-6
We note that this unbelief belonged to the town, to the people in general, and not any particular individual. Amazingly this seemed to actually prevent Jesus performing any miraculous work.

In Mark 8:22-26 Jesus takes a blind man out of the unbelieving village, Bethsaida (see Matthew 11:21), before restoring his sight. He then sends him home, instructing him to avoid the village, as the unbelieving people there may have poured scorn or doubt on the miracle he had received.

Then in the account of the healing of the boy in Mark 9:14-29 we see unbelief operating at three different levels:
*Individually in the boy's father (v24)
*Corporately in the nine disciples (see Matthew 17:19-20)
*Culturally in the unbelieving generation' (v19)

We must tackle and defeat unbelief, bringing ourselves and others to a faith-filled position. We need to recognise and confront it on three levels.

Individually: In ourselves first and then with those we seek to release healing to. We read the word, hearing it as faith comes by this means (Romans 10:17). We praise God, declaring His goodness and power, and remain impressed with Jesus, not intimidated by illness. We recall and announce the good news of testimonies of healing in Jesus' name. We repent (change the way we think) of unbelief and break any agreement or alignment with it. We ask the Lord if there is any root cause of unbelief in us that needs to be uprooted.

Corporately: This is especially relevant in the church. We should not expect to find faith among those who are not Christians, though sometime we do! A local church is a community of faith, but sometimes unbelief, and other strongholds have found their way in among us. That does not mean all those share the same mind on this, but the unbelief, even of a few can greatly hinder the flowing of the Spirit's power to heal. We take the same steps to counter this as with the individual. Teaching of the word with revelation and insight from the Spirit will go a long way to break this power of unbelief.

Culturally: This is of course much more difficult to address. However, as the church moves forward bringing healing in Jesus' name, so the praise, thanks and testimony of the Lord will increase in our land. This may seem like a gradual trickle coming against a might dam, but it will make a difference.

Offence and unforgiveness

Again, in Mark 6:1-6 when Jesus encounters resistance in His home town, part of the problem is that the people take offence at Him. Offended hearts cause stumbling and are maybe the greatest detriment to living in God's grace and fullness.

A brother offended is harder to win than a strong city, and contentions are like the bars of a castle. Proverbs 18:19

Jesus made it abundantly clear that we must forgive those who wrong us so we can benefit from the forgiveness of God in our lives (Matthew 6:12,14-15; 18:21-35; Mark 11:25).

Unforgiveness is a common blockage that we need to address in bringing healing to people. It is vital people understand the damage they do to themselves by withholding forgiveness, and that to forgive is a decision of the will, not a feeling. Releasing forgiveness to one who has wronged you has the effect of breaking the hold they have over you. We have often witnessed people come into great healing after they have declared and released forgiveness, even to those who have grievously wounded them, and sometimes, even after the death of the one who inflicted the wounds, declaring forgiveness was still liberating.

Any breakdown in relationships has an effect on our health, and disunity among God's people hinders His healing river from flowing among us. Reconciliation is a necessary process to bring and release more healing in our lives and into the world.

Root Issues

Many who come for healing presenting a physical condition have a root cause that is not always apparent at first. In Mark 2:1-12 a paralysed man is brought to Jesus. In healing the man, Jesus first declares, 'Son, your sins are forgiven.'

Root issues can be many and varied – common ones are abuse - often as a child; trauma; fear of many kinds; grief and loss that has not been worked through; rejection issues, and other emotional wounding. It is important to address these as the person is willing and the Spirit leads.

If we don't address these roots, we can find ourselves speaking words of healing and seeing no fruit, but becoming increasingly disappointed and discouraged. However, when we take time, listening well to the person involved and to the Holy Spirit, we can see wonderful fruit as these blockages are unblocked and great freedom and healing comes. If we don't see healing coming, then always ask the necessary questions: Why not? Is there any blockage?

One day we ministered to a lady who was in a great deal of pain, walking with two sticks, and suffering from insomnia. There seemed to be no clear physical reason for her condition so we asked as Jesus once did, 'how long have you been like this?' Her reply of 'around six years' led to the follow up question of 'what happened around six years ago'? She told us how her son had been tragically killed in an accident six and half years before. We discerned that the terrible grief over her son had been trapped within her and was showing itself through all these ailments. We therefore prayed words of release from grief and she gave it over to Jesus. Release came, followed by a profound and deep peace from the Lord where she lay motionless for some fifteen minutes. She got up feeling quite different. I met her about a month later, though had to look twice to check it was the same person. Now looking about ten years younger, she told me she had no pain, no sticks and slept well every night.

As we deal with these root issues, we do need to be aware of the possible attachment of demonic spirits in these areas and the need, at times, for deliverance ministry. Remember that of the specific individual healings recorded in the gospels, Jesus often dealt with a demonic root (see Mark 5:1-20; 7:24-30; 9:14-27; Matthew 9:32-35; 12:22-24; Luke 13:10-17). While we should never assume that any condition is caused by a demon, we must be aware that it could be, and be ready to deal with this if necessary.

Persevere: The Need to Press In
We see that many of Jesus' healings were instant and some were more of a process. However, what do we do when nothing appears to be happening? (While we often do see signs of healing taking place, there are a good number of occasions when nothing seems to be happening visibly yet healing is taking place). There is always a need for persevering in all things and healing is no exception. We don't 'heal the sick' because it works but because Jesus tells us to and send us. So, we are not to be put off when nothing seems to happen. We stand on the word of God and keep standing.

Like the mother in Matthew 15:21-28, who pressed through the obstacles that even Jesus and His disciples seemed to put up, we keep coming back, worshipping, believing, and holding firm to His word.

Though the nine disciples were unable to heal the boy in Mark 9:14-29 they press in to Jesus and ask the important question: 'Why couldn't we drive it out?' They knew this could work (they had cast out demons and healed people before), and should have worked, so they wanted to gain understanding of why it hadn't happened. It is vitally important that we never give in to a sense of failure but run back to Jesus to seek Him for greater understanding.

A Good Practice of Healing

While there is no formula for healing, and we need to be led by the Holy Spirit, there are good steps to take in line with what we see Jesus doing.

1. **Ask** – what do you want? Encourage the person to be specific. Do you believe? Cultivate faith. Will you receive? Help them to be as receptive as they can. We find people more receptive as they stand.
2. **Discern** – any blocks and how to proceed. What type of healing is needed first? Does there appear to be anything hindering them receiving healing? Deal with any blockages you can at this point, though more may surface as you continue.
3. **Engage** – speak blessing and healing to the person in Jesus name. Lay hands on sensitively (though not always necessary), and speak as the Spirit leads in line with God's word. Don't talk too much – Jesus often just said, 'Be healed!'
4. **Assess** – observe and ask what's happening? Any change? Continue as appropriate.
5. **Advice** – what to do now? Give thanks for what God has done or maybe recommend more prayer if needed.

Announcing good news, undoing the works of the evil, and healing the sick are the three main kingdom expressions we see in the ministry of Jesus and His disciples. They all bring life, joy and peace. It is our privilege and responsibilty to receive this for ourselves and then release this to others.

Response

Have a look at these passages from Acts and write down what you learn?

8:4-8

_____

_____

_____

_____

9:32-40

_____

_____

_____

_____

14:8-10

_____

_____

_____

_____

28:7-9

_____

_____

_____

_____

Is there anything in your life that is hindering you receiving healing from the Lord?

_____

_____

_____

_____

What steps could you take to become more active in releasing healing as a sign of the kingdom of God?

_____

_____

_____

_____

_____

_____

_____

PART 4: BREAKTHROUGH: BIRTHING AND BUILDING

For the LORD will rise up as at Mount Perazim,
He will be stirred up as in the valley of Gibeon,
To do His task, His unusual task,
And to work His work, His extraordinary work.
Isaiah 28:21

Enlarge the place of your tent,
and let the curtains of your habitations be stretched out.
Isaiah 54:2 (ESV)

Those from among you will rebuild the ancient ruins;
You will raise up the age-old foundations;
And you will be called the repairer of the breach,
The restorer of streets in which to dwell.
Isaiah 58:12

These verses from the prophet Isaiah speak of breakthrough, of birthing and of building. They call for extension, expansion and the extraordinary. They invite us and challenge us into something beyond.

BREAKTHROUGH

Isaiah 28:21 speaks of two places – Mount Perazim and Gibeon. Perazim means the breakthrough, coming from the word to breach and to burst through. It was a place of victory for David over the Philistines (2 Samuel 5:20). Gibeon was also a place of extraordinary victory where Joshua defeated the Amorites, as the Lord miraculously extended the day to allow for a complete routing of the enemy (Joshua 10:10-12). This was indeed a strange occurrence, and Isaiah emphasises the unusual and extraordinary works of God. We find a similar term in Acts 19:11 where God 'performed extraordinary miracles by the hands of Paul' to bring about significant breakthrough in the city of Ephesus. These works are not what we have been used to or familiar with, but go beyond. The Lord will rise up and be stirred up for extraordinary and exceptional works. His eyes range throughout the earth looking for those who will respond to His call to join Him in these breakthrough adventures and activities.

BIRTHING

Isaiah 54 opens with a promise to a barren woman who has no children, calling her to shout for joy because of the birthing that is coming. This declaration to the nation of Israel still calls out to us today. In anticipation of new births, we are both to rejoice and to prepare a dwelling place. It is a call to stretch in readiness to go beyond. No parents would bring a new born baby home and then start thinking about buying a cot or other essential utensils. They would have done this beforehand; they would have got prepared because they knew the birth was imminent.

BUILDING

Finally, Isaiah 58:12 speaks of building and raising up the old foundations. This building in readiness for God's extraordinary work is not raising up what we have done before, but going back to Biblical foundations. The church, the household of God, is built on 'the foundation of the apostles and prophets, Christ Jesus Himself being the corner stone' (Ephesians 2:20). We must always build aligned to the corner stone that is Christ, and we still need the apostolic thrust fuelled by prophetic encouragement. This will lead to the repairing of where the enemy has breached the walls. That repairing is the intercessory role of standing in the gap so as to protect and keep the harvest that God gives. Lastly, there is the restoring of streets, literally paths, in which those born of the Spirit can dwell, being nurtured and built up into maturity.

STEPPING OUT

What now? What next?
If we only ask 'what next' then we can keep dreaming of great things but may never actually step into them. It can be all too easy to dream and talk of what might or could be, and while this dreaming with the Spirit of God is good, we can falsely satisfy ourselves with a dream that never becomes reality.
So, we also ask 'what now?'

In 1999 we sensed the Lord calling us to step out, leaving pastoral ministry to pioneer new works. Moving out of the church manse, and having no set source of income, we trusted the God who calls, to provide, and so began an amazing adventure of watching His wonderful and faithful provision for us over the next seventeen years.

We first pioneered Prayer for the City in Glasgow, followed a few years later by beginning Healing Rooms in Scotland, and planting a new church along the way. We travelled some unfamiliar paths, learning all the time to lean more fully on the Lord. We witnessed His faithfulness to His word, and at times miraculous works as walked on His unseen realities.

The Spirit begins to stir in us. We may not understand what is going on but something is happening and we know that much. Then He plants His seed into us and something is conceived in our heart. That which is conceived from the Holy Spirit, if carried to its full-term, will birth an extension of the ministry of Christ here on earth.

The kingdom of God is increasing; our heritage in the Lord is to bear much fruit that will remain (John 15:5, 16); and Jesus declares, 'the harvest is plentiful' (Matthew 9:37). The harvest needs equipped workers who will go announcing and demonstrating His kingdom. The great catch requires mended nets and the aid of many boats. The increase calls for a readiness of widely stretched out tent curtains.

10. BUILDING WITH JESUS

Jesus famously said, "I will build My church" (Matthew 16:18) or did He?

The word 'church' is both a wrong and unhelpful translation of the Greek term 'ekklesia' which is found in the New Testament. It comes from quite a different root and has led to much misunderstanding.

The ekklesia was 'a group of citizens called out for governmental purposes.' This included military strategy and election of magistrates. They could also be a small group who listened to and recorded what the king/emperor said and acted to see his will implemented.
The parallels seem clear – we are citizens of heaven living on earth, called together under Christ for the purpose of implementing His will/kingdom on earth as in heaven. We of course do this in a quite different manner. This is what Jesus is talking about in the only two times that He uses the term – Matthew 16:13-19 and 18:15-20. In both passages Jesus refers to 'binding and loosing' suggesting this is a primary purpose of His ekklesia.

So, what does that look like for us? What are we binding and what are we loosing? Essentially, we bind what God binds and loose what He looses, and loose what Satan binds and bind what Satan looses (e.g. Luke 13:16, John 11:44). This activity of binding and loosing opens the way for much greater effectiveness for the good news of the kingdom to spread.

There has been a little confusion and ignorance over this subject. We need to understand the importance Jesus attached to this and the order of the way things work. Whatever has been bound or loosed in heaven (past and completed act) shall now (present and future) be bound and loosed by us as Christ's ambassadors on earth. Tom Marshall in his booklet *Binding and Loosing* says: "The decisions of earth follow the decisions of heaven. The activities of earth follow the activities of heaven. The judgements of earth follow the judgements of heaven. The declarations of earth follow the declarations of heaven." God initiates; we follow. This is the role of intercessory prayer that we looked at previously.

Jesus also stated the importance of 'binding the strong man' before taking away his goods and plundering his house (Mark 3:27). Jesus has defeated Satan and the powers of darkness on the cross. When people receive the exchange of life that the cross brought, then the strong man is bound and we can legally enforce Christ's victory in their life.

When the ekklesia of Christ operates in the authority He has given us, then the strong man is restricted and we can loose the words and works of the kingdom on earth. We will explore more of what we mean by 'church', but it is essential to recognise this primary definition and purpose that Jesus gives to His people.

NEW TESTAMENT PICTURES OF 'CHURCH'
The Body of Christ (Ephesians 1:22-23; Colossians 2:19): Jesus is the head, or source, and we all together make up His body on earth, fulfilling various functions and actions under His direction.

The Family (Household) of God (Ephesians 2:18-19): Relating to God as the Father of the house, we seek the best for one another, building each other up in His love.

The Temple (Ephesians 2:20-21; 1 Corinthians 3:16-17): Not a physical building, but a spiritual dwelling place for the presence of God.

The Bride of Christ (Ephesians 5:25-27): Betrothed to Jesus in an unbreakable covenant we await the wedding feast of the Lamb. We relate to Him in intimacy as the bride who He has made holy and spotless.

The Army of God (Ephesians 6:10-13; 2 Corinthians 10:3-5): There is a warring purpose for the people of God here on earth as we displace the rule of darkness with kingdom of the Son.

None of these images fully define the church. They are all aspects of who we are and call out differing responses to the Lord. Essentially, we are the people of God, called out of darkness into His light; a treasured possession that He has taken for Himself; a covenant people among whom He walks. We are not the church in isolation from each other, but when we meet, we are the assembly of the saints who release the kingdom reign of God on earth.

NEW TESTAMENT MODELS
Jerusalem: We can learn much from the first church established in Jerusalem. We see some key components and aspects of their shared life (Acts 2:42-47; 4:32-35). The apostles teaching all that Jesus had commanded them; the practice of prayer and the praising of God; eating meals together; sharing with any in need, and a sense of awe at what the Lord was doing among them. There was a clear commitment to the Lordship of the Risen Jesus; to generosity; and an expectation to witness the power of God.

This assembly in Jerusalem also had its challenges, outward opposition and inner strife which they had to resist. But their weakness seems to be that they did not willingly follow Jesus' instruction to go out to Judea, Samaria and the ends of the earth, and it was only through persecution that they were scattered beyond.

Antioch: Something shifted in Antioch! While the scattered believers proclaimed Jesus wherever they went, they still focussed on the Jewish people only. Peter had his breakthrough moment of revelation and took the message to Cornelius' Gentile household in Acts 10, but there still had not been a wholesale going to the Gentiles. We see this in Acts 11:20 where the scattered ones went 'speaking the word to no one except Jews alone.' However, the next verse tells us that there were some who began to speak to Greeks also. The Lord was clearly with them and they saw a great work of salvation (Acts 11:21-24). This breakthrough birthed and built a mission-based church where Paul and Barnabas would teach and then be sent out from (Acts 11:25-26; 13:1-3). It would become Paul's mission base that he would return to and be launched out from once again.

Ephesus: Paul would establish several churches, sometimes staying a very short time and at other times a bit longer. He stayed in Ephesus for three years as this became his equipping base. He not only had established new churches, but now he equipped men and women to go and plant many new churches. He taught daily to those in the city and to the people from surrounding towns and villages who would have come into Ephesus for business and other reasons. It was also a place of spiritual battle, being the stronghold of the goddess Artemis (or known as Diana). But with the witness of great miracles Paul established this training headquarters for the whole region.

The New Testament ekklesia which assembled to bring the kingdom of God on earth, was a family or household who shared in a common life, often expressed in sharing meals together; a house of prayer that bound what was bound in heaven and loosed what had been loosed in heaven; an equipping centre where all followers of Jesus were made ready and trained, and a mission base from which they launched out from to announce good news, demonstrate the kingdom, and make disciples who then came into the family.

STRETCHING WIDE THE TENTS

In response to Jesus' statement of an abundant harvest, and His promise that those who abide in Him will bear much fruit, what are we to do?

Our mission is not to form some sort of church; our mission is to announce good news and make disciples. A community of faith, a church, is the result. If we focus on building a church, we don't often get disciples, but if we focus on making disciples, we will get church.

We need to grow into harvest minded people and develop the means for reaping and keeping this fruit of Christ's sacrifice. We can do this in many ways; within our present church expression and by birthing and planting new expressions.

Meals and Miracles

Most of us have homes and we all eat! A meal around a table in a home is one of the most natural expressions of shared life as a family and with friends or neighbours. One of the greatest and simplest gifts is the gift of hospitality. The early church ate together – a lot! They also witnessed the working of God's power in miraculous ways. The combination of a simple meal and the release of the power of God to move on people's lives is a wonderful one.

Jesus welcomed the crowds, spoke to them of the kingdom of God and healed those needing healing – then he fed them (Luke 9:11-17)! These are the necessary ingredients. A genuine welcome that values people and affirms them. Then we can feed them as we are not in a remote place with little food and a huge crowd. As we eat, we talk about life, about the kingdom of God, and the testimony of Jesus. Then we let Him walk among us, healing, bringing peace, prophecy, wisdom and much more. God's people are blessed and those who are not yet believers are drawn to Him. This meal table is also a natural place to begin a discipling journey.

Planting 'church'
What is your image of a church plant? What is needed to do this?
Many think of buildings and budgets and you maybe don't have either. But you don't need either. The believers met in homes and Paul hired a hall.

If we look to replicate much of what we already have as church then we are missing a huge opportunity. The complexity of much of what we call church – the building, an office, staff, structures, and programmes – are not the essentials that we read about in the early church. These things are not wrong in themselves, and in certain situations are helpful, but this is not what we should aspire to or feel we would have to have if we started a new church.

We can aim instead to keep it simple. Church life is sustained by relationships more than by structures or programmes. People want relationship; we were made for relationship. It can also be small and grow and multiply.

It starts with the stirring of the Spirit of the Lord who then sows His seed, plants His idea, and something is conceived in us. There is then a battle to carry it to birth. A battle with self-doubt, and with sceptical and scornful voices disdainfully asking, 'who are you to do this?' A battle with the enemy of souls who seeks to deceive us into apathy and inactivity.

We must listen to the voice of the Lord. He asks (Exodus 4:2), 'what is that in your hand?' and the prophet asks (2 Kings 4:2), 'what do you have in the house?' The widow replies, 'nothing except a jar of oil,' but is instructed to gather as many jars as she can because the oil will never run out while there are jars for it to fill.

Fresh wineskins and New Wine

We have the new wine of the Spirit and it must be poured into fresh wineskins so it won't be lost. We need both though. There is no point in coming up with some fresh wineskin, no matter how great it looks, if you don't have the new wine of the Spirit. God is both refreshing His church and producing some new, fresh wineskins.

What does this freshness look like? Living in the freedom of the grace of Christ; flowing in the wonder of worship of our God in spirit and truth; and moving in partnership with the power of the Holy Spirit. These flow over into our relationships as we share in this common life in the love of the Father, and in our witness to the world with the good news and the goodness of God.

Response

What is the Spirit of the Lord stirring in you?

_____

_____

_____

_____

_____

What does He want to conceive in you for you to birth?

_____

_____

_____

_____

Who might you partner with in birthing and building?

_____

_____

_____

_____

_____

11. LEADING WITH JESUS

If we are to be a means of breakthrough to something more; birthing something with the Holy Spirit, and building something with Jesus, then we need to learn to lead His way. New works, whether great or small require leadership. Someone must go before as a forerunner. Someone must lead the way whether on familiar or unfamiliar paths. Someone must take the helm and steer the ship.

Definitions of Leadership:
"Leadership is influence, the ability of one person to influence others to follow his or her lead." J. Oswald Sanders
 "Leadership is the capacity and will to rally men and women to a common purpose, and the character which inspires confidence." Bernard Montgomery
"A leader is one who knows the road, who can keep ahead, and who pulls others after him." John Mott
"Leadership is about creating the conditions in which other people can thrive." Nigel Wright
"Follow Me" Jesus

Leadership is essentially about influence. We are influenced by someone and we will all influence someone else at some point. A good leader recognises who and what has been influencing them, and chooses wisely who and what they will allow to influence them from this point on. A follower of Jesus wants His influence in their life so they can influence others accordingly.

TOP TEN LEADERSHIP PRINCIPLES OF JESUS (John Maxwell)

1. Leadership is servanthood (Matt. 20:25-28)
2. Let your purpose prioritise your life (Matt 6:33; Luke 19:10; John 17:4)
3. Live the life before you lead others (Luke 7:22-23; John 14:11)
4. Impact comes from relationships, not positions (Luke 9:6; John 4:5-30)
5. Leaders must replenish themselves (Mark 1:35-38; 6:31)
6. Great leaders call for great commitment (Matt. 10:17; Mark 8:34-38)
7. Show security when handling tough issues (Mark 11:27-33; Luke 20:19-26)
8. Credibility comes by meeting needs and solving problems (Luke 5:12-15; 8:35-39)
9. Leaders must choose and develop their key people (Mark 3:14; Luke 10:1)
10. There is no success without a successor (Matt. 28:20; Acts 1:8)

What do you see in the leadership example of Jesus?

_____
_____
_____
_____
_____
_____

What qualities do you look for in a leader?

_____
_____
_____

_____

_____

_____

Do you see those qualities in your own life? Which ones?

_____

_____

_____

_____

_____

Keys of character and integrity

Integrity builds trust, and trust builds relationships. We are leading people forward in the ways of the kingdom of God. We are first and foremost leading people not an organisation, so we lead in a personal manner. It is much easier to lead people with whom you have a healthy and current relationship. We build up credit with people, so if we make a mistake or if we have to confront them over something, then it is done from a place of credible relationship.

Healthy relationships are built on trust which usually takes time to build. People trust someone who they believe they can rely on, who is consistent, and who lives a life of integrity. That is a whole and complete life, not a life that behaves one way in one situation and another way in other circumstances.

Godly character and integrity come out of our relationship with the grace of Christ and the love of the Father. Here we know who we are in Him, where we have nothing to hide, prove or fear. We can then lead out of this security in the Lord.

Healthy leaders motivate rather than manipulate. Guilt seems like a great motivator to get a person to give money or do something, but it produces no real lasting fruit and is ultimately oppressive. Lazy leaders use guilt as a shortcut but ultimately lose out as people see through them and move on.

We lead out of who we are, and what and who has influenced us the most. Jesus led from being the Beloved Son with whom the Father was well-pleased. We can and must lead from this same grace given basis.

Leadership Keys

1. **Foresight:** We see ahead, we see what's coming and the opportunities, possibilities and challenges that await. We can prepare and be ready. Great visionary leaders may have this ability, but all of us in Christ have the huge advantage of the leading of the Holy Spirit, the ultimate visionary.

2. **Vision and goals**: We receive vision that then needs to be translated into goals. We need to bring it down to earth, where the rubber hits the road. Good leadership is the ability to impart vision so others can embrace it.

3. **Timing:** Knowing when to act is crucial. A difficulty for 'forerunners' is that they see ahead, they see what's coming. It feels like this should be present to them, but other people haven't seen it yet, and they are not ready to run with it. Knowing what to share and when to share it and with whom are all vital. As momentum begins to happen then recognise this and use it well. John Maxwell says, 'Momentum is the leaders best friend.'

4. **Coping with criticism and stress:** Going out in front means the risk of being shot at! Not everyone will like what we say, or see what we see. The world is full of opinions, criticism, blame-shifting, and offended hearts. Leadership that makes

a difference will bring great fruit but also invite opposition and criticism as it did with Jesus. The key is not to seek to avoid this but to learn to deal with it in a healthy way that furthers growth. Once again, living according to the grace of Jesus Christ is our key. Stress can strengthen us if we use it well, and criticism can keep us in check if it comes in the right spirit.

5. **Leaders initiate instead of reacting:** We can react to people, to their comments of praise and criticism, or we can live in response to God. We can live in reaction to what is going on around us or we can be those who initiate God's creative ways into our world.

6. **Problem solving:** Anyone can see problems, and many can describe and analyse them, but true leaders find and bring solutions. Developing an ability to solve people's problems will endear us to them as leaders. The world is full of problems, but God has solutions. He gives wisdom to find His solution in different situations we find ourselves in.

7. **People empowering:** Good and godly leadership enables other people to thrive and rejoices in their fruitfulness. We lead people into their potential rather than using them to exalt ours. We show people what to do and how to do it.

Keys of personal development:

John Maxwell says, 'Leadership develops daily, not in a day.' Some people appear to be born with a great gift for leading others, but even that needs continually developed. We all have an ability to lead, and for most of us we have to develop this day by day. It is a work in progress, and we can progress.

1. **Self-discipline:** Some people shun discipline as restrictive, but self-discipline and freedom go hand in hand. Good self-discipline enables us to focus and not to be distracted by many things. Mary was self-disciplined in sitting at the feet of Jesus (Luke 10:38-42), which then naturally led her to that place at Jesus' feet in her time of trouble (John 11:32). Developing good self-discipline frees us from the procrastination that puts off and misses opportunities.

2. **Fostering the right relationships:** Who we spend time with, listen to, and thereby allow to influence us is really important. Psalm 1 warns us about walking, sitting and standing with the wrong people (Psalm 1:1). Instead, we want to build and cultivate relationships with those who sharpen us, encourage us and challenge us to go further. These relationships rarely just happen, but need to be identified and built.

3. **Keeping priorities but not having too many:** Do less, accomplish more! Know what your mission is and keep focussed. List your priorities for this time. We should not have too many or try to spread ourselves too thinly. Keep to them and don't get side-tracked by lesser things or demands. Jesus didn't give in to people's demands or popularity but kept His priorities of time with the Father and preaching the kingdom (Luke 4:42-44).

4. **Persevere:** Again, we see that perseverance is such a vital quality and practice. Learning to lead well takes practice; battling through opposition needs determination; building good relationships requires time and effort; and developing any work in the kingdom involves a willingness to pay the price and persevere through whatever comes.

Leading from under good leadership

Good leaders release and empower others to lead well. If we are to lead well, we need to be led well by someone else. Just as we can only exercise authority in Christ when we live under His authority, we can only lead well when we are both under His leadership and the leadership influence of someone or some people with whom we have been put into relationship.

An important passage of Scripture in relation to this is found in Ephesians 5:18-21. Verse 21 along with the following verses have been mistranslated and misused to keep others (especially wives) in submission. However, we must recognise two important factors about the meaning of Paul's words.

First, the word translated as 'subject' or 'submit' was a military term which meant to arrange troops in a military fashion under the command of a leader. It is never about control in an oppressive sense, but aligning together in an effective way. It is not about ruling over someone but being arranged in the best way to overcome together.

Second, the command is not to submit, or be subject to or even to align. The command in this whole passage is found in verse 18, and that is 'to be filled with the Spirit.' The consequences of being continually filled with the Holy Spirit is that we will speak and sing to one another and the Lord, giving thanks and being subject or aligned to one another in reverence of Christ.

Being aligned with leaders who we can fit well with and receive instruction from will benefit us enormously. Being submitted to them enables us to receive from them and together become more than we could be on our own.

We are commissioned or sent out by the Lord and by others. Paul, or Saul, along with Barnabas were called apart by the Holy Spirit and then sent out by the other leaders at Antioch (Acts 13:1-3). They would return to Antioch and give account of their ministry. There was an accountability. This is important, but again has been misused at times. To be accountable is to be answerable to someone or some group for what we are doing, and when necessary to be challenged and corrected, but it is not to be seen in a restrictive light. The word actually means to give an account for your ability. Therefore, those we are accountable to should be looking to make sure we are living and operating to the fullness of our ability. It is not so much checking up on us to catch us out on any mistakes we make, but to encourage us to go further, and to maximise our potential in the Lord at this time.

Building Team
In the book of Acts, we discover team ministry: what we might call apostolic teams that were sent out from the churches. Paul starts with Barnabas, but when they have a sharp disagreement (and that can happen), they part ways and each takes a new partner. Over time we see Paul's teams change and grow in number (see Acts 20:4). These teams are not permanent, but come together for a long or short time for a particular purpose.
In forming and building a team there are certain qualities to look for:

Faithful: We want faithful people who will stick with us and with the task.

Available: That may not be a 24-7 availability but there must be the right availability for the purpose for which the team has come together.

Teachable: We need people who are willing to learn, not those who think they know it all. People who are also willing to unlearn some things to be trained in new ways.
We can work with and develop people even from a quite immature starting point if they show the above qualities.

Jesus carefully and prayerfully selected His team (see 6:12-16). He didn't call for volunteers, and while He welcomed all who came to

Him, He didn't just put anyone on His team. If we get the right team to begin with it can save a lot of pain in having to remove someone from the team if they show themselves unsuitable.

As we develop a team, we must likewise be faithful and available to them. We teach and train them, and this will largely come through what we model to them. People learn and grow largely through what they see and are released to do themselves.

MOTHERS AND FATHERS

For if you were to have countless tutors in Christ, yet you would not have many fathers, for in Christ Jesus I became your father through the gospel. Therefore, I exhort you, be imitators of me.
1 Corinthians 4:15-16

The Lord is after sons and daughters who can mature into fathers and mothers. We can't be mature fathers unless we have learned to be sons. Even if that didn't really happen for us in the natural family life, it can happen in the Lord and through spiritual fathers and mothers.

Paul is saying that there may be very many who teach and instruct but there are few who truly father and mother people in the Lord. Teaching is of great value, especially when it comes with insight and revelation, but it has a limit. There is something that only fathers and mothers can impart. There is a level of affirmation and nurturing that requires parenting. We can listen to teachers but we will imitate fathers and mothers. There is a great need for godly, mature spiritual fathers and mothers who are worthy of imitation.

The reversal of the potential curse at the end of the Old Testament (Malachi 4:5-6) comes by turning the hearts of the fathers and the children to one another. We see in our world the damage, indeed the curse, that comes when these relationships are missing, abusive or unhealthy.

Paul's images of mothers and fathers in his ministry: 1 Thessalonians 1-2

1:6 'You have become imitators of us and of the Lord'
2:7 'But we proved to be gentle among you, as a nursing mother tenderly cares for her own children'
2:8 'Having so fond an affection for you, we were well-pleased to impart to you not only the gospel of God but our very lives, because you had become very dear to us'
2:11 'exhorting and encouraging and imploring each one of you as a father would his own children'

The Father and Mother blessings

Fathers and mothers who love us are designed to release their blessing to us. To affirm us in who we are, to nurture the life and potential within us, to give us permission to thrive and flourish, and to encourage us all the way. Spiritual fathers and mothers can do all this. We can be good spiritual parents even if we haven't been natural parents, or if we feel we made mistakes in the natural family. What we need is to be sons and daughters who are truly fathered by the Father, then we communicate His heart to others.

Great leaders lead by example; they are worth following and imitating. They invest in people, drawing out the best in them. They invest in relationship and build teams. They enable and empower others to act. They walk in integrity of heart and can be trusted. We can all become great leaders through the example, enabling and empowering of Jesus Christ.

Response

Which of the definitions of leadership did you relate to the most?

_____

_____

_____

Why?

_____

_____

_____

_____

_____

What areas of leadership could you work on to become a more effective and godly leader?

_____

_____

_____

_____

_____

_____

What will you do to develop in these areas?

_____

_____

_____

_____

_____

_____

12. BELIEVING WITH JESUS

All things are possible to him who believes **Mark 9:23**

What is possible?

We can live as new creations in Christ in the freedom of His amazing grace.

We can know and experience the wonderful love and blessing of the Father.

We can partner with the Holy Spirit, being filled with His power to witness to this new life in Christ.

We can behold the Lord, being transformed into His likeness.

We can hear from God and speak prophetically.

We can stand in the gap bringing forth the will of God on earth through prayer.

We can announce the good news backed up by the demonstration of signs and wonders.

We can take authority over the power of the evil one, undoing his works.

We can heal the sick in Jesus' name.

We can bring breakthrough; birthing new ministries and building with Jesus.

In Him we can. And more – there's always more!

As we are renewed in the spirit of our mind, we see what is possible; we see from heaven's perspective. The key is believing.

Believing with Jesus, believing with the faith of the Son of God. Not a faith we manufacture or hype up, but His faith, believing what Jesus believes, and believing as He believes.

We are being equipped 'for the work of service, to the building up of the body of Christ; until we all attain to the unity of the faith, and of the knowledge of the Son of God, to a mature man, to the measure of the stature which belongs to the fullness of Christ' (Ephesians 4:12-13). Wow! This is what God is doing in equipping His sons and daughters. And when we grow together into that unity of faith, in an increasing knowledge of Jesus, more fully impressed with Him, into maturity and the full measure God has for us in Christ, then together we will move beyond where we have been and into the vast territory of Paul's blessing in Ephesians 3:20-21:
Now to Him who is able to do far more abundantly beyond all that we ask or think, according to the power that works within us, to Him be glory in the church and in Christ Jesus to all generations forever and ever. Amen

Blessed to be fruitful and to multiply

Immediately before He ascended to heaven, Jesus raised His hands and blessed His disciples as he was sending them out as His representatives (Luke 24:50-51). The last act of Jesus on earth echoed the first act of God when He created us:
God blessed them; and God said to them, "Be fruitful and multiply..."
Genesis 1:28
Let's read this slowly, a phrase at a time:
#God blessed them – think about what that means from what we have learned about blessing. It wasn't just a nice word, 'O bless you!' It was affirmation, impartation, permission. It was calling them up to be who He intended them to be and to enter into all that He had planned for them.

#God said – He spoke, His words of spirit and life resounding into their being. His voice stirs our souls, awakens us fully, calls us to attention, and directs our way.

#Be fruitful – hear this word to you! This command, this invitation, this challenge! Receive the permission it gives you. Let it lift you up into God's intention for your life. Let it release you to go and bear much fruit.

#And multiply – yes, more of you in the world, more of us! The world will be much better off with a multiplication of Christ followers, of lives that have been impressed with Jesus.

Those disciples received Jesus' blessing, got filled with and fuelled by the Holy Spirit, and launched out into God's plan and will to become fruitful people who multiplied throughout the nations.

We must cast off the clothes of disappointment and its accompanying fear. We must reject the bar of low expectation. We must not bow down to the cultural trends that would silence us. We must believe like Jesus, and suffer with Jesus, and press through to lay hold of that for which He laid hold of us.

Breaking through
As we step out and up, get ready. There will be challenges, there will be blows and buffeting. As soon as Jesus experienced the Father's voice at His baptism, He was thrust into the wilderness to have His Sonship questioned.

As soon as I was accepted to train for ministry by the Baptist church in Scotland, Helen was struck by a deep, dark and debilitating post-natal depression. Five long and difficult months followed before God broke in and that depression fled. (You can read Helen's story in her book *The Day that Changed My Life*). During the years of my training for ministry our families were struck by untimely and tragic deaths, including both Helen and I losing brothers who were only in their twenties. As I was called to be pastor of my first church a split occurred in the congregation with over one third leaving. We felt the refining fire of God upon our lives.

Many years later I would journey through a wilderness season where I felt empty and it seemed to me that maybe the Lord had finished with me. A deep sense of vulnerability brooded over my life, and there seemed no clear sense of direction. There aren't many signposts in the wilderness and I experienced a deep sense of disorientation. Even our financial position looked unsteady for the first time since we had stepped out many years before. But God was at work!

In my vulnerability He was birthing a deeper trust; in my disorientation He was bringing a re-orientation. As this time was nearing an end, I felt we needed a holiday. I did something I wouldn't normally do and booked a trip on our credit card, not knowing how we would pay it. A couple of days later, as I heard the post drop through the letter box, I simply knew in my spirit that was our cheque! I opened a card which contained a cheque for £1,000. The card read, 'To Steven and Helen, this is for you to have some fun!' It was from someone we did know, and when Helen called to thank her, this dear lady told her that she had actually been writing that cheque to another ministry when she sensed the Lord say to her, 'Steven and Helen need that!' A simple story but it made a huge difference and still moves me.

The road to bringing spiritual breakthrough can be narrow and filled with trials. Yet it is the most awesome adventure where we discover the faithfulness of God and witness the break out of His mighty works. He invites and challenges each one us to travel this adventurous kingdom path that He has for us. Your path won't be the same as mine, but ultimately our paths will converge into a rushing river that flows with the testimony of Jesus, the goodness of God, and His life-transforming Spirit.

Now the God of peace, who brought up from the dead the great Shepherd of the sheep, through the blood of the eternal covenant, Jesus our Lord, equip you in every good thing to do His will, working in us that which is pleasing in His sight, through Jesus Christ, to whom be the glory forever and ever. Amen Hebrews 13:20-21

Response

Write out as best you can express it:
What do you believe Jesus Christ has laid hold of you for?

_____

_____

_____

_____

_____

_____

What will you do now to seek to lay hold of this?

_____

_____

_____

_____

_____

_____

_____

Steven Anderson has been involved in a variety of Christian leadership roles since 1987. Steven was pastor of a Baptist Church before he, and his wife Helen, together formed Prayer for the City in Glasgow. In 2004 they pioneered Healing Rooms in Scotland which they led for 10 years.

They have written several books including *Releasing Healing, Life to the Full, Discovery Questions* and *The Day That Changed My Life.*

Printed in Great Britain
by Amazon

63744290R00088